BLOODSPIN

J. Beresford Hines

Relentless Publishing House, LLC
Columbia, SC

RELENTLESS
PUBLISHING

BloodSpin

Copyright © 2019 by J. Beresford Hines.

Published by :

Relentless Publishing House, LLC

www.relentlesspublishing.com

RELENTLESS
PUBLISHING

ISBN: 9781948829939

First Edition: November 2019

10 9 8 7 6 5 4 3 2 1

BLOODSPIN

The screenplay follows the lives of a few military women, who were labeled suicide victims and the journey of a bathroom matron who is launched into the 19th-century medical community's alleged medical advancement in its research of African American female patients and cadavers".

(BLOODSPIN)

INT: CONGRESSIONAL FEMALE BATHROOM DAY

IT IS AN ELABORATE WOMEN'S BATHROOM. THE FLOOR IS WHITE MARBLE AND THE FOUR BOOTHS ARE NAVY BLUE. THE SINKS AND ADJACENT LIFE SIZE MIRRORS ARE DRESSED IN RED AND GOLD. ABOVE EACH STALL IS A SMALL GOLDEN CHANDELIER. ON THE FRONT
OF EACH DOOR IS A `USA SYMBOL FOR THE CAPITOL BUILDING. THE WALLS IN THE BATHROOM ARE WALL PAPER OF THE CONSTITUTION AND REPLICAS OF THE AMERICAN FLAG AND ALSO HAS THE SYMBOL H-211 SURRONDING THE ROOM.THE FAR RIGHT IS ANOTHER BOOTH WHICH IS PEARL WHITE AND HAS A SIGN ON IT WHICH READS ATTENDANT. CLOSE
TO THE DOOR ARE SOFAS AND CHAIRS AND A TABLE WITH FEMALE TOILETRIES. THERE IS SOFT SWING JAZZ PLAYING IN THE BACKGROUND. OLIVE EXITS FROM THE ATTENDENT'S BOOTH. SHE IS DRESSED IN A WHITE UNIFORM AND IS VERY ATTENTIVE TO THE BATHROOM. SHE IS DUSTING, SPRAYING AND PREPPING EVERYTHING FOR THE PATRONS. SHE EVENS SPRAYS HERSELF. TWO WOMEN ENTER THE BATHROOM. ONE GOES TO THE SINK AND LOOKS IN THE MIRROR. THE OTHER QUICKLY ENTERS A STALL WHILE UNDRESSING.

> OPESH
>
> You're suppose to wait until you get in the booth before you
> start pulling your clothes off!

ROPE' speaks from the booth

> ROPE'
>
> Any later I'd have to stay here all night washing out this dress.

Opesh washes her hands, Olive is grabbing paper towels and subserviently walks over waiting to be acknowledged.

> OPESH
>
> I'm just glad we finally got a bathroom that was closer to the
> chambers. My husband doesn't believe we had to walk to the
> other side of the building just to tinkle.

Rope' exits the booth and goes to the sink. Olive gets more towels and still stands half bowing near the women waiting to be acknowledged. Opesh lunges her hand down the sink then slumps to the floor.

ROPE'

What wrong?

Olive inches closer

OPESH

My wedding ring! My ring just rolled down the drain.

She fingers the sink again, to no avail.

ROPE'

OK! Ok, what time do we have to be back in the chambers?

OPESH

My husband will never believe me. He'll swear I gave to an intern or some other lawmaker.

ROPE'

Look, the attendant is here. She must know how to get things like this out.

For the first time the women make eye contact with Olive and motion for her to approach.

ROPE'

You saw what happen. Can you get the ring out?

OLIVE

Lord willing ma'am.

Opesh gives a frustration sigh.

OPESH

I'll give you a big tip, if you get that ring back. It's my wedding ring! When are you going to get started? We have to return to our meetings. Olive hands the ladies the paper towels. They semi-snatch them. Wipe their hands and leave them on the sink. Olive goes to her booth.

ROPE'

Don't act as if you haven't given the ring away before.

They look at each other sarcastically. Opesh waves her hand at her friend.

> OPESH
>
> We have grown. We're communicating better. . .

Opesh addresses Olive again.

> OPESH (CONT'D)
>
> We know a lot of people in the Capitol building once you get that ring out.
> We could talk to somebody for you.

Olive returns with some tape and begins taping around the sink and also blocks off the sink with cones. Opesh is becoming furious at the inaction of Olives strategy.

> OPESH
>
> Why are you doing this?

Opesh pointing to the items Olive is using.

> OLIVE
>
> Yes ma'am, I have to block it off till I can get to it, because other ladies
> might come in.

Rope' goes over and taps Olive's tip dish.

> ROPE'
>
> She just doesn't want to miss out on any loose change.

All the women exchange glances. Olive remains subservient, almost blowing the truth in these circumstances.

> OPESH
>
> I told you I'll take care of you, once you get that ring. I want you to do it
> now! I'll buy you a whole new dish!

> OLIVE
>
> If the Lord see fit to do it to ma'am.

Rope' and Opesh shakes their heads in frustration. As they exit, they speak to each other but overheard by Olive.

OPESH

I detest the traditional churched, who believe God intended them to be poor and subservient to everyone.

ROPE'

As long as God tells her to get that ring out, I'll tip her.

The bathroom door closes quietly and Olive pulls a chair from her room and sits in front of the sink. Pulls out tools from her apron and begins to work. There is an eerie silence within the bathroom. Only sound is Olive's tools in the sink. She looks around her surroundings. There is reddish smoke seeping from all the mirrors simultaneously. Olive stands and steps back against the booths. The room darkens and the mirrors smoke more. She is frightened and walks towards the main bathroom door. Looking back, Olive stiffens by boots exiting from the mirrors.

She slips inside a booth and peeps out watching as three female soldiers exit from the mirrors, each is representing different branches of the military, yet their uniforms are tattered and destroyed. They are bleeding and blood is dripping everywhere. Their faces have scars and holes in their heads and bodies from bullet and trauma wounds. They also have been set aflame and their complexions are charred. Some of their clothing has been ripped near their genitalia indicating forced entry. There is also an odor, which causes Olive to hold her nose from the stench. All three military personnel stand in front of the mirrors looking in Olive's direction. Olive exits slowly looking more at the floor and mess than the women.

OLIVE

You messed up my bathroom! Why are you here? Who are you?

The character's voices are shattered, frighten and hurting.

MOLFAIR

Afghanistan! Financial unit. No fire just paperwork and supplies. The bills got paid! There was a party, male and female. I never made it. It's under investigation. I have a gunshot wound to the back of my head, my uniform is burnt, I smell like gas, and I've been sodomized. The report says I did this to myself. How is that possible?

Molfair looks to her left then straight at Olive, sizing her up and down. Another speaks.

GELINE

I was an online college track star. I wanted to join up since 911. I love America. I hate Iraq, but look at me now. I was a virgin. Someone ransacks my virginity; they took my eyesight. I remember sleeping in my bunk, then waking up roadside naked, gagged and grenaded. I wish I was home. Yet, the report said, I did this to myself. How is that possible?

Geline looks to her left then at Olive, another speaks.

> RUETT
>
> I wasn't afraid to be me, to love who I love, and tell anyone about it. The guys hated me but they had to listen to me. They couldn't stand I could compete with them. I got my daddy's height, feet and thighs, yet I was an angel like my mother, but I couldn't show it. This macho assignment. I hate insecure men and women, so what they were threatened by me. I was a strong woman in this man's war. Never thought it would happen to me. The report said I did it to myself. How could I knife myself through my own liver, bleed, shoot off a round to my face and no one respond?

> RUETT (CONT'D)
>
> Set a tent on fire, while I'm bleeding, tie and gag my hands and pour gas on my breast and vagina. How could I do this to myself? I guess I got myself pregnant too!

Olive continues to look at the mess that was made. She grabs her bucket and mop and begins mopping. She continues looking downward at the floor instead of the spirits. Olive speaks, but refuses to look up.

> OLIVE
>
> Why are you here with me? Yawl got to go back from where you came. Some ladies will be coming to use the bathroom and yawl going to make me lose my job, if this place is not spotless.

> RUETT
>
> We are here because you are here and you are one of us. A woman.

Olive shakes her head in defiance.

> OLIVE
>
> I ain't none of yawl. I don't know what you young girls are today. A woman doesn't wear men clothes, out there trying to be the hunter, when you should be hunted. No man wants to chase a train that ain't running.

GELINE

Grandma, look at us. We are somebody's sister, daughter, wife, auntie, and friend. Do you think we like being like this? We are hurting. Our families are crying. Our churches been praying and nothing is happening.

OLIVE

I ain't your grandma and don't go throwing the church at me, even if I believed you, no self-respecting church girl would lie about all that you'll said happened to you. Stuff happen during wartime.

OLIVE (CONT'D)

You'll signed up for this. You could have stayed home and been somebody's wife or been a schoolteacher.

MOLFAIR

I wonder if I could smack her although I'm dead. She doesn't want to help us.

Ruett holds back Molfair from attacking Olive.

OLIVE

What makes you think I can help you if you are dead? Yawl just messing up the bathroom. This is H-211. This the capitol building they just built for the women. Yawl sure you are at the right address?

Molfair smacks the air toward Olive. Olive feels the breeze and backs up a little but still refuses to acknowledge them.

RUETT

You have to tell somebody we were here.

OLIVE

Then you need to go over to the men's bathroom and tell some men. They might do something about it. They got wives, daughters, sisters and mammas. I don't get involved.

GELINE

We are ladies, we've always been ladies and we don't go in men's bathroom. Women understand women, we understand each other.

OLIVE

No, we don't!

RUETT

You remember your first bra? The first time Aunt Flow came to visit?

RUETT (CONT'D)

Have you ever been to a Gyn? Men don't understand that.

OLIVE

I don't have an Aunt Flow. No, I don't go to the gym and I still have my first bra.

Molfair unstraps her revolver and is about to un-holster it. Geline motions for her to stop.

MOLFAIR

Perhaps, I could shoot her just a little?

RUETT

Nope, that's woman on woman crime. We in death have to warn life, because those in life are doing too much of nothing.

MOLFAIR

How are we going to reach this chick? What's wrong with her?

GELINE

Why you hate us Gma?

Olive continues mopping up blood and debris as it continues to drop from each character.

OLIVE

Don't hate nobody, but I ain't the somebody you should be asking.

GELINE

If you're not helping, then maybe you're hating us.

OLIVE

I ain't no man! This is where I am. I work here in the Capitol building bathroom. I've been here a long time, at least four presidents. Nobody bothers me. I don't bother nobody. I just let the ladies come do their business. I'm just waiting on retirement. What's wrong with yawl? Every time I mop one spot and go to another, the other spot got blood on it again?

GELINE

Gma we need you. As long as there are women dying overseas, blood going to spill here too.

Olive freezes and looks at them.

OLIVE

What do I have to do to keep this bathroom clean? All of you are dripping everywhere!

MOLFAIR

You see what she asked! She just concerned about the bathroom and her job. She doesn't care about us or the other women! Let me leave her with a little scar!

RUETT

We running out of time. We don't have the time to visit someone new.

OLIVE

Listen to her. Yawl have to go on up out of here. I didn't know the dead keep time. Why you can't visit anybody else?

GELINE

Our time is up. Although we dead, we still dying. Each time one abused woman dies, we all die. We visit you till you figure out what to do.

Olive lowers her head and continues mopping as if it's going to make a difference.

OLIVE

I ain't that smart. I'm here. I know me. I can't be bothering people when they doing their business here and upstairs.

OLIVE (CONT'D)

I bowl. They play tennis and golf. I like collards. They like kale. They come here to make a deposit. They don't want to leave here with no withdrawals.

The spirits rip off their name tags and drop them on the floor. They pull out other name tags of other women from their pockets and toss them around the bathrooms. All of the tags are blood soaked.

MOLFAIR

Now you have more to clean up without any excuses!

Molfair turns and leaves as does the others in formation. Each exiting the mirror they entered from. The smoke follows them and the lights rise. The room is still soiled and Olive mops, cleans and gathers the name tags. She barely looks at the mirrors but shines them anyway. The name tags she toss in a trash can clearly marked file 13.

The bathroom door burst open. It is Opesh and Rope'.

OPESH

Ok little missy. You've had enough time to get the ring, where is it?

Olive just raises her hands and walks over to the covered sink.

OLIVE

No, ma'am, I haven't had time. I just finished cleaning . . .

ROPE'

Cleaning? This is a new bathroom, there haven't been enough women in here within the last two hours for you not to have been working on the sink. I think you got it and not going to give it to us.

They walk toward her. Olive backs up a little.

OPESH

We won't tell anyone, just give us back the ring.

OLIVE

I haven't got your ring ma'am. I just been busy.

ROPE'

We could call a plumber.

Olive rapidly interjects at the thought of a man coming in to do her job.

OLIVE

No need for a man to be in here. This is a woman's place!

OPESH

Then get my ring woman! I'm thinking you stole it and holding it to either sell it or use it against me.

OLIVE

I'd never, I don't know how . . .

ROPE'

You from the south right?

Olive suspiciously nods her head.

ROPE' (CONT'D)

Some southernisms say if you lie, you'll steal and you'll cheat which one are you?

Olive shouts.

OLIVE

I always tell the truth. I don't have nothing to lie about. Your ring is in the sink. Go check for yourself!

OPESH

Don't need to, that's your job!

Olive goes over to the sink with the ring in it she grabs a coat hanger from her tool bag, then moves the can of blood tags away from the ladies but the rattling of the blood tinged name tags catch the ladies' attention. They walk over and peak into the can, as Olive tries to hide them near her.

ROPE'

What are you trying to hide from us? Is that someone's tampons?

The ladies react, becoming almost nauseated and gaging at the blood in the can. They quickly back away and staring at Olive angrily.

> OPESH
>
> Sick, you're just sick. You've been here too long.

> OLIVE
>
> No, no, it's not mine!

> ROPE'
>
> I should hope not. I know your groceries already have been delivered!

> OLIVE
>
> No, no, I have to tell you about some other ladies that were here. They left these here!

Olive runs over and grabs the trash can and attempts to show the women, but they scatter away from her.

> OPESH
>
> Olive, you need some help! You're holding on to other women's stained napkins, that's sick! You better not get any blood on my ring!

The women dart for the bathroom door, but Olive shouts at them and they freeze leaning on the door.

> OLIVE
>
> These are name tags! Not tampon, name tags!

Olive attempts shows them the tags again, but is reluctant to place her bare hands in the bucket.

Olive reaches into her apron and grabs a paper towel pulls one out a name tag, but it still resembles a used tampon as blood drips on the floor. Olive wipes it with a paper towel.

> OPESH

Why would you have blood stained name tags in this bathroom? It has to be tampons!

           ROPE'

Never mind that! Why do you have so many?

           OLIVE

They came from the mirrors. The blood came from the mirrors.

Olive points to the mirrors and both women attentively walk past Olive watching her closely and then view each mirror and only see their own reflection. They walk toward Olive and help her put the trash can down, not looking into the trash can again. Reluctantly put their arms around her and try to escort her from the bathroom. She rebels.

Olive shoves the two women away from her. She realizes they think she is insane and are placating her not comforting her.

           OLIVE (CONT'D)

I can't leave!

           OPESH

WHY? Why?

           ROPE'

We have someone in our chambers to help you with problems like this

Olive sits down on the sofa; the ladies sit down also on opposite sides but not close.

           OLIVE

I can't leave. My shift is not over. I don't need help.

           ROPE'

Yes you do!

OPESH

I'm not sure where you got gross sight from and believe its name tags,
but it doesn't sound right. Ok just stay here. We need to leave, we'll be
back, be a doll and work on getting my ring out without the blood.

The ladies look at each other and quickly exit. Olive stands and begins working on the sink. She glances back at the mirrors and the front door expecting someone to break her silence. The set darkens again as before. Olive hides again and peaks out of the stall. The spirits exit the mirrors again. Ruett motions for Olive to exit the stall, she does so reluctantly.

OLIVE

They won't believe me! You should get somebody else; a man would be
so much more forceful.

RUETT

Is that what you think of yourself?

MOLFAIR

You didn't say anything to defend us!

OLIVE

I can't, I shall not, it's just the way it is life goes on, I did would I could . . .

GELINE

Why are you so bitter and tentative to us woman?

Olive goes into her cleaning mode again, ignoring them and cleaning the bathroom that continually gets soiled from the spirits blood, dirt and clothing.

OLIVE

My life is my life, are you not here for yourselves and others? My life my
life to be left alone.

MOLFAIR

You had better tell them about us!

Tell them about the women raped! Killed, transported, or I'll transport you.

Olive locks eyes with Molfair for a second and then Ruett steps between them.

RUETT

I heard you say you were from the south?

Olive slightly nods her head and looks around as if she doesn't want anyone to hear.

OLIVE

As southern as you can get?

GELINE

I don't hear any accent Gma?

OLIVE

It gone now, now that I've put some years on.

MOLFAIR

Do we have to go through this, let me inside her!

Olive backs away looking at all three of them surrounding her.

RUETT

Stand Down!

Molfair backs away from advancing.

RUETT (CONT'D)

We'll wait on that!

MOLFAIR

We're running out of time playing with this woman! Just don't
understand why a woman won't help a woman. Other women knew I
was targeted, they had to know. Other women knew the uppers wanted
to trash me, they knew I was missing, they put a shade over my sunshine,
a cover over my head. They even typed the report on my life so my
parents would limit the questions to Uncle Sam.

Geline looks at her companions, and excludes Olive from the conversation.

GELINE

She's right, we have to do this ourselves.

OLIVE

Do What?
Molfair gives Olive sharp look.

MOLFAIR

Why are you interested Man!

Olive shocked by the comment.

OLIVE

I'm not a man!

MOLFAIR

You want to be, you wish you were, you wish you were in control, and
dictate what you want a woman to do. You said a man could do a better
job than you. What's right with you!

Olive goes back to her cleaning and moping, Molfair kicks the mop-stick from Olive's hands and it skids away
from her. Molfair follows Olive. A startled Olive and runs and attempts to picks it up again. Molfair's footsteps
on the mop-handle holding it to the floor. Molfair still is provoking Olive to retaliate.

RUETT

I said stand down Molfair!

Molfair release the mop-handle and Olive slowly picks it up. Reluctantly she answers.

> OLIVE

What do you want me to do?

> GELINE

More than you've done, it's not enough to tell you've got to show them.

> RUETT

Everything under investigation. That's a code word for let truth twist. Like a centrifuge and disappear.

> OLIVE

What can I show them from here, I can't leave here, I've been here, it's my job, it's my life, it's who I am.

> GELINE

Shut the front door!

Molfair looks and her pitifully.

> MOLFAIR

You alive we're dead! We had a future, opportunities! We stuck with you!

Olive shifts more away from Molfair's anger.

> GELINE

Why are you so stuck to this place, it's a bathroom? It can stink in here.

> OLIVE

I lived in one, gave birth in one I the baby was born with no heartbeat. Something else happened, my urine and my feces leaked from me, it stunk, and no one could be around me. I hated myself. I exiled from myself. I felt I could exit in a bathroom where no one expects much of me and the smell of me blends.

MOLFAIR

We can't smell anymore, remember we're dead but if you don't do something to help you still can stink!

GELINE

Are you still leaking?

OLIVE

The hole was repaired, but I know it has not repaired in my head.

Olives sits on the floor exhausted. The spirits sit around her except Molfair who angrily paces the room checking and eyeing Olive and preparing for intruders, always on alert. They all look at her with a wondering why moment. Molfair glances at everyone and with sarcasm responds.

MOLFAIR

Somebody has to stand guard!

GELINE

We're stateside!

Molfair stomps her boots angrily.

RUETT

She's like all of us, Alert fatigue.

MOLFAIR

Right here in this building there is a war going on! We sure can pick them, we're dead and she can't leave the bathroom!

GELINE

How are we going to make them remember?

OLIVE

Who?

MOLFAIR

Who do you think we talking about chocolate girl?

Molfair's seething anger staring at Olive.

RUETT

America!

MOLFAIR

American Women!

Olive rises and starts cleaning the commode and other areas that are stained.

RUETT

The same way they let our families know we wasn't coming home. We counter-centrifuge. Olive we're running out of time.

Olive looks at the spirits questioning.

GELINE

We can do but so much, we given our blood, our unborn children, our families monies, our lives and time. Our families were given our tears for shadows of truth. Olive, you got to counter centrifuge for us.

RUETT

The women raped in war, dying from noncombat and abuse causalities. All in file 13, on a desk, a yesterday, a second ago, a minute a go, five minutes ago, twenty minutes ago, a week ago, a month ago six months ago, a year ago and a war ago. It's spinning blood!

OLIVE

Why are you laying all of this on me? I'm no lawmaker, they upstairs in the chambers go haunt them. All I have is these and this is where I am.

Olive holds up her hands with the paper towels and mop. The spirits slowly and methodically slowly attempt to reenter the mirror. Olive goes back to cleaning.

OLIVE (CONT'D)

Where will you go? Are you coming back?

Olive a little concerned, the ignore Olive enter the mirror silently, never looking back, except Molfair

MOLFAIR

It shouldn't matter to you where we go, only to us because we're dead
and now we're gone. We know women die in war, but not our way. You
understand me woman!

Olive nods her head. Molfair puts her finger inside the bullet wound in her head and then splashes blood on Olive, then angrily charges at Olive and stops.

GELINE

Never knew nobody that didn't have a wound.

MOLFAIR

Just wanted to spill a little blood to go to remind you of the sisters that
didn't make it!

Olive frantically wipes the sprinkles of blood off her face, mouth and clothing, using the cold-water faucet to remove stains. Molfair enters her mirror along with the other spirits and Olive cleans up behind them, this time cleaning the mirrors. Before she cleans the final mirror, a body bag is tossed out. Olive slowly peels down the zipper and screams and shouts at the sight of body parts, in a frantic she drops some of the opened body parts in to a series of empty trash cans, but realizes it's not working then zips it up the bag. Olive still tries to clean up the blood she spilled, but she is overwhelmed.

Olive is on the floor distraught at the site, she moves away from the bag and looks around her environment. She takes off her shoes and tears her uniform.

Olive goes in and out of the stalls and slings toilet paper and flush each toilet with wads of paper until the commodes over flows.

She runs to the main door and locks it from the inside with her key then moves the couches, chairs and furniture in front of the door. No one can enter. She grabs a hammer from her tool bag and hammers at the sink and destroys it, keeping the mirror in tack. She is out of breath. Then she sits in her chair.

There is a knock outside the door.

INT/EXT: OUTSIDE THE BATHROOM DOOR.

The scene moves back and forth between inside and outside the bathroom door.

> OPESH
>
> Olive! Why is door locked? This is not your home, this bathroom belongs to the women of the United States Senate, and we demand that you open this door immediately!

Olive remains still, staring back and forth between the body parts and the mirrors. Rope' and Opesh speak to each other outside of the bathroom.

> ROPE'
>
> You think, the woman is still in there, she might be in that stall of hers reading, she might have taken the ring and left.

> OPESH
>
> She said she can't leave, her shift is not over, go get somebody to open this door.

> ROPE'
>
> You go, I really do have to pee, like yesterday.

Rope' bangs harder on the door. Opesh jets away. Rope' twist and hops waiting for a response.

> ROPE' (CONT'D)
> Please miss lady, the other lady with the ring is going to get someone to open this door and you're going to be in serious sugar. I'm about to wet all this floor outside this door.

INT: BATHROOM

Olive quietly tiptoes to the door.

> OLIVE

You really have to go?

Rope' gets excited and braces herself against the door for the sudden rush in.

> ROPE'

Sure, I do like rain on a roof.

> OLIVE

Back away from the door, so I can see your shadow from underneath the door.

Olive is on the floor looking at the shadows or movement underneath the door.

Surprised Rope' does back away and the door unlocks quickly, Olive quickly ushers out the number 13 trash can, then slams the door shut.

> OLIVE

Like rain in a can!

Rope' is shocked, but twisted around anxious to go. Rope' turns and looks around the room and prepares to squat then looks cautiously into the can and gasp. Rope' speaks to Olive from outside the bathroom door.

> ROPE'

Are those napkins still in here?

Olive for the first time looks back at the series of cans and then realizes she gave the wrong trash can to Rope'. Olive swallows hard. Rope' screams, pulls up her panties and backs away against a wall. Opesh runs up, look at Rope's frantically!

> OPESH

What's wrong with you, screaming like that do you want secret service down here! Security is on their way! You wouldn't believe what I had to go through just to get people to believe me, that we had a bathroom on this side of the building. Much less explain that we were locked out by the matron. It's been a joke on the senate floor.

Rope', just keep screaming and whimpering and pointing to the can. Opesh has to calm her down by holding her harms down and holding her like a child.

> OPESH
>
> Did you use the bathroom?

Rope' somewhat relieved but stutters when she speaks.

> ROPE'
>
> Don't have to go no more, maybe ever. Look in the can!

Opesh vacillates back and forth. Rope' points several times for Opesh to look.

> OPESH
>
> You didn't use that can to relive yourself, did you?

Rope' dramatically shakes her head no. Opesh walks over to the can and gags at the site, and drops to her knees.

> OPESH (CONT'D)
>
> My God! My God what has this woman done in there! We have to call the police, find out whether anybody is missing in the building!

Opesh calls for help on her cellphone, behind the door Olive listens, then shouts.

> OLIVE
>
> Find out if any more women are missing any . . .

Opesh shouts back through the door.

> OPESH
>
> Olive why are you doing this? These are body parts why are they here in this trash can! Who are these people?

> OLIVE
>
> Shouldn't you have been asking me for your ring? I thought that was your only concern!

> OPESH
>
> You do know you will be prosecuted to the full extent of the law for these crimes!

> OLIVE
>
> And who are going to put these women's lives back together? Will you just investigate and flush everything between their births and deaths like the paper you finish using inside the commode?

Opesh looks back at Rope' who's still in shock with her back against the wall. Opesh holds up her hands at Olive's speech. Opesh looks at Rope' hoping to gain some composure. Rope is still in a stoic, but responsive state.

> OPESH
>
> She's deranged, what's taking security so long?

> ROPE'
>
> I'm clueless.

Olive again speaks through the door, this time a little more forcefully.

> OLIVE
>
> So is America. When a daughter, a wife, a mother, a sister, or a woman, dies from abuse, especially, at the in war or out of war it gets blanketed. BloodSpin!

Olive is surprised and ashamed at what she just said. She covers her mouth to silence her speech. She can't believe what has happened to her.

> OPESH
>
> Olive you will be arrested and sent to jail. You are holding the bathroom hostage and destroying a room in a federal building. Once this is resolved and this quiet's down, everything will go back to normal. What is it you are trying to prove and what are your demands?

Rope' silently mouths to Opesh with her arms open for clarity bathroom hostage? Opesh just shakes her head at the spare of the moment thought.

Olive sits down on the couch and looks around at her destroyed bathroom. She stands and she goes to each mirror, she looks through it and places her head on each, there is a loud thump against the bathroom door. It is an ax splitting the wood. Olive stands near the door and screams out.

OLIVE

COUNTER-CENTRIFUGE! COUNTER-CENTRIFUGE!

Olive looks at the main door and then looks behind her at the destroyed bathroom, she walks toward each mirror and looks intently at each one as the hammering continues.

Olive looks at her hands and is still mystified she sits on the floor, her hands spread, Olive then stands and walks toward the mirror climbs over the debris and gingerly steps into a mirror.

Olive enters the mirror and is immediately catapulted into the 19th century. She cannot be seen by anyone; however, she feels the heat and senses the stench of the current environment. She unbuttons her top button and fans herself with her hand, while simultaneously holding her mouth and nose from the odor.

ENT. PLANTATION 19TH CENTURY LANDSCAPE

A large Victorian house is surrounded by acres of well-manicured land.

The sounds of an early morning southern city permeate the atmosphere. The house has white marble steps with enormous egg shell pillars that dominate the landscape. Several white women dressed in layered Victoria dresses enter and leave the facility, each shadowed by their parasols from the searing sun. Engraved in the pearl marble above the cocoa colored door is the name of the physician Wolfgang Coop gynecological research.

INT. DOCTOR'S OFFICE

A white doctor dressed in a man of means 19th century clothing is in a room with a female white assistant. He is about to examine a white woman with her travel clothing on. With extreme reverence and looking glass in his hand, he very discretely motions for the woman to hold up her dress, (never looking at her directly but respecting her dignity). He is resistant to invading her privacy and has not asked her to disrobe at all. After a quick glance with his magnifying glass, he sees what he needs then pushes her dress down. He moves away from her and addresses the patient.

DOCTOR COOP
Ma'am' pardon the intrusion, since your delivery of the child recently, it
seems that the opening has created an additional opening. We are in the
experimental stage and we are creating a remedy to help you get back to
being a wife and mother.

> WOMAN
>
> Thank you, Doctor Coop, but I'm still in pain! How shall I fulfill my
> husband's needs, when it's quite difficult and pain-full?

Doctor Coop wipes his hand on a used towel, and stands and smiles at the women authoritatively and pats her on the hand.

> DOCTOR COOP
>
> I will speak to your husband right away young lady as you prepare yourself to
> depart.

The doctor abruptly leaves the examination office as the woman and the doctor's assistant help her with her clothing.

I/E. DOCTOR'S OFFICE WAITING ROOM

The waiting room is immaculate; there are other female patients waiting anxiously together as their husbands converse with other men adjacent room but within earshot and eyesight. As Doctor Coop enters the room, a young man quickly stands and greets him with a handshake and inaudibly Dr. Coop whispers something in his ear and they both smile. Doctor Coop secretly hands a small ether bottle and handkerchief to which the young man shyly inserts it into his inside jacket pocket. The young man's wife enters the room then he puts his hand around her and they exit. Dr. Coop waves the next patient to the examination room.

EXT- SAME DAY-EVENING, ON THE STEPS OF HIS CLINIC

Doctor Coop waves goodbye to his patients as their horse and buggy gallops away. He walks around to the back of the house, untying his tie and rolling up his sleeves.

In the middle of the field, at least 500 feet from the main house is a large dreary Spartan wooden building. Each window is covered from the inside with burlap allowing minimal light to enter. Just as he about to enter the door, ANARCHA (female slave) opens the door and cowers downward as he enters.

INT. BARN BUILDING

Coop barely acknowledges her. Anarcha quickly helps him disrobe his morning attire and places a blacksmith's apron upon him and with two-hands gives Coop doctor's tool bag. Coop then waves his hand in the air and Anarcha quickly departs and trots subserviently around the room lighting each station with an oil lantern.

Olive's spirit enters the room. She has been observing, not knowing why she's here, just following her curiosity. Olive looks through the dimmed light room at 11 different stations. The lights become clearer as she steps closer. It is a makeshift hospital room. Each station is identical to the other. The cot's sheets are reddish brown lightly washed, there are also patients silently asleep laying in varied positions. All slave women, each lying in fetal, prostrate, supine, sideways, over-the-edge positions in a silent effort to relive pain.

Olive gasp in disbelief and slowing backs herself in a corner as Coop heads in the direction of one of the patients. Olive hovers more in her corner waiting and watching.

DOCTOR COOP

I need everyone awake!

Dr. Coop looks at Anarcha to make this happen! Anarcha claps her hands loudly and nudges the women. She throws freezing water on unawaken patients and each patient shouts with mild whimpers from the response of the water.

DOCTOR COOP (CONT'D)

The other physicians will be here momentarily. Forget the others. I just need one, right now. If she is not awake soon, I'll use you!

At the thought of that, Anarcha moves quickly to the nearest young girl and shakes her violently, although, semiconscious she awakens. The girl attempts to say something, but Anarcha motions for her to remain silent! Just as Coop approaches her, the front door opens and several white physicians enter with their bag of tools and dress the same as Dr. Coop. They each assemble around the young woman in a semi-circle. Dr. Coop enters the center. Anarcha subtlety exits the group tending to the other women, keeping them silent, while covering their mouths with her hands.

DOCTOR COOP (CONT'D)

Doctors, thank you for coming at such a late hour. Our reputations as physicians and researchers from across the nation are at stake! We are obligated to exercise our right to discover things about the female anatomy that traditionally has not been explored. Although, our research here does not truly explore the dominate culture, we'll have to use lesser example to help our women in the future.

Coop waves for the other physicians to surround the teenager to hold down her arms and legs. She starts squirming and kicking immediately. Shrieking and screaming at high and lower tones until tears start leaking into her ears. The victim's eyes pierce into each physicians' eyes pleading for assistance. Each physician diverts their gaze toward Dr. Coop who covers her upper torso and examines the infected area. The patient's thighs are extremely apart causing her legs muscle to spasm at the stretching. Coop speaks as an orator addressing a crowd to the physicians.

DOCTOR COOP (CONT'D)

Gentlemen, as a result of this slave's recent child birth, as well as, the other slave subjects, who I have purchased for our experiments.

DOCTOR COOP (CONT'D)

All the slaves have a tear in their vaginal areas, which has caused the
urine to leak into the vaginal arena and rectum causing great difficulty,
pain and odor.

Coop waves his hand over his eyes and nose at the stench and continues speaking.

In quest for the advancement of medical education, white men and our wives who have this problem will thank us as our success increases. I will undertake the experimenting and eventually repairing of this condition in this landmark surgery!

Coop reaches into his bag and methodically, yanks out a typical smaller size butcher knife. Someone hands him a flame which sears the blade until it white heat sizzles from Coop's mouth's vapors. The victim is screaming as the doctors increase their grip on her. Some also engaging their knees and legs to steady the patient. One doctor approaches and holds the lantern for Coop at a distance away and lights the vaginal area. Another physician looks away as Coop takes the burning tip and slices the burning fragile flesh.

ANOTHER PHYSICIAN

Sir! Her screams are thunderous and they would wake up the dead!
Why on God's green earth have you not anaesthetized this young
woman?

In the midst of cutting, the blade still searing the flesh,
Coop glances in his direction while the child continues to shriek.

DOCTOR COOP

No worries. Outside of a light wail, no one can hear us for miles. Slave
people do not feel as much pain as our culture does. Besides, she wasn't
the loudest.

Coop pauses and grabs some nearby towels and soaks up the blood and fluids profusely flowing from the victim's vaginal area. Coop stands and looks in the direction of Anarcha pointing toward her. All the men look in her direction, Olive is standing in the shadow, although she is a spirit, she still cannot be seen. She shudders backward thinking the white doctors can see her. She stumbles what she thinks is a broom, but it is Anarcha's foot.

Anarcha's notice the bump to her foot, but ignores it because her attention is on her Master's voice and his pending request. Coop addresses Anarcha.

DOCTOR COOP (CONT'D)

Show the good doctors why you no longer my loudest crier?

Anarcha doesn't understand what request is made of her. She stands there wanting for direct orders but is confused.

DOCTOR COOP (CONT'D)

Open your mouth! Open your mouth!

Quite embarrassed, Anarcha does so, revealing a mouth full of white teeth minus the tongue. The other doctors are immediately stunned.

ANOTHER PHYSICIAN

Her tongue is gone!

DOCTOR COOP

Gentleman, let us not forget, slaves are our property. Anarcha's voice was entirely earth shattering and I continued to hear it in my sleep. It had to done! I'm at peace.

The men return to the hemorrhaging patient. Anarcha silently tip-toes away to a medication table, unbeknown to the physicians, whose backs are to Anarcha. Only Olive watches Anarcha's movements.

Anarcha puts her back to the edge of the medication table and her eyes watch the physicians. Behind her like a precise pharmaceutical specialist she pours and feels the different size pills, and reinserts them back in the enclosure, searching for the right size. Once she's located the correct size, she takes two white pills, quickly inserts them in her mouth and swallows.

The searing of the flesh stops, and each physician helps or hands a primitive surgical item to Coop. After several minutes of attempts to stop the bleeding and the urine flow with towels, the floor below the patient is saturated with blood. Coop is literally sewing flesh with a primitive needle and string. Coop stands back and looks at his work.

DOCTOR COOP (CONT'D)

Doctors I believe we conquered much today. It seems the bleeding has decreased somewhat.

Coop dabs a blood tinged towel at the area as blood continues to drop to the floor.

ANOTHER PHYSICIAN

Could you be certain, with so much swelling? Does infection become
a factor?

Coop lightly touches the swollen area and there is slight pop. Blood, infection and the strings are primed to burst.

Coop senses the damage is occurring and covers up the young teen who has fainted earlier from the pain. He times her pulse for life taps and covers her up to her head, then taps on the head.

Coop makes his way toward the next station with the other patients lying frightfully upon the cots.

DOCTOR COOP

Doctors! Here's what we have learned, that we have to consider
many factors during surgical repair. Thus, how do we get to Carnegie
Hall?

In unison all of them shout out, laughing amongst each other.

OTHER PHYSICIANS

Practice, Practice, Practice!

Coop then uncovers another patient to conduct the identical experiment.

At this time, Anarcha has slumped down to the floor in a nod from the pills she has taken. Olive looks at the physician's first victim, the pending victim and Anarcha. All are bewildered. Olive speaks aloud, though no one can hear her.

OLIVE

Lord Jesus, why you got me here?

Olive scans the room searching for a mirror, yet only sees reflections in brass items. She looks at the medication table and slowly turns to read the jar of pills Anarcha took. It reads opium/morphine. She again looks at Anarcha.

OLIVE (CONT'D)

Lord Jesus! Help me, help them!

DOCTOR COOP

I need someone to give the slave we just finished with two opium. I don't
need her to awaken right now or during this surgery.

Another physician heads toward the medication table. Olive slightly steps away. He grabs two pills, places them in a crushing jar and proceeds to crush them. Then places them in glass of water and proceeds to the previous patient, who is unconscious. He attempts to wake her to get her to drink, with no success. The new physician is dumbfounded.

>   ANOTHER PHYSICIAN
>
> Doctor Coop sir, it seems she won't awaken in order to take the
> concoction.

>   DOCTOR COOP
>
> Think, first year!

Dr. Coop says this sarcastically. The physician searches and finds a funnel and hose. He then positions the first patient at a 45-degree angle for gravity purposes with towels. Then proceeds to empty the contents in the funnel. Once it's empty, though slight spilled, he allows her head to drop without much concern.

>   ANOTHER PHYSICIAN
>
> Dr. Coop how many surgeries have you done?

Coop pauses for conversation, as he again lights the flame and heats up the small butcher knife.

>   DOCTOR COOP
>
> Overall, I've done quite a few on my slave's children, who were sick
> because of how filthy they are. The parents were too lazy to clean up.
> Therefore, I had to do multiple surgeries on infants that had some
> infections. I used those tools on the wall to adjust the newborns skulls.

Coop nods towards a series of different sizes corkscrews on the wall.

>   DOCTOR COOP (CONT'D)
>
> There is scientific evidence that slave skulls grow quicker, than ours and
> I attempted to give it more space for the brain to grow.

>   ANOTHER PHYSICIAN
> How successful were the surgeries?

>   DOCTOR COOP
>
> I punctured a few scalps, although the modification seems to work.

>   ANOTHER PHYSICIAN
>
> And the infants?

DOCTOR COOP

I thought the long-term investment of surgery on women is more profitable and notable than continually purchasing young slave infants and have them die on me.

ANOTHER PHYSICIAN

Thank you, Dr. Coop, however, I was referring to your experiences with the surgery we are witnessing now.

Coop speaks as we hear the woman scream at the sewing and cutting of flesh.

DOCTOR COOP

Oh! Right now, I'm working on my thirty-third case, despite continued complications.

Coop nods to the previous patient.

OTHER PHYSICIANS

How are the other patients fairing since the surgeries?

DOCTOR COOP

You can ask them yourselves. Number 31 just got the opium. This patient we're working on is 32 and the other can't talk.

ANOTHER PHYSICIAN
How many surgeries has she had?

DOCTOR COOP

The experiments don't matter! Anarcha is my initial subject. In order to perfect the repair of this ungodly circumstance, we have to use what is available. Her thirty experiments are nothing in the name of medical advancement!

EXT. DAY OUTSIDE OF THE BARN BUILDING

Dr. Coop and the other physicians gather around for an early morning smoke and customary goodbyes. Coop locks the door then heads for the plantation office and home, as the other physicians get into or on their horse carriages and leave the area.

INT. BARN BUILDING

Olive circles each low-lit medical station, eyeing the women. Some still bleeding while other are heavily sedated. Some of the women have fainted and are lying in excruciating pain, whimpering softly so not to draw attention to themselves. None see Olive as she is frustrated at her attempt to touch them, but her hands just flow through each one without response.

Olive returns to Anarcha, who's is in a slight stupor from the opium, but not able to function. Anarcha looks in the direction of Olive and frighteningly waves at her and tries to move, but cannot. Olive waves back and moves toward her. Anarcha moves in the opposite direction and tries to scream, but nothing exits her mouth except a grunt. Anarcha faints to the floor in a sitting position. Olive continues to approach and walks across Anarcha's legs, then returns back the other way. Olive then sits next to Anarcha and her own body positions exactly like Anarcha's as if they were both looking at a mirror together. Olive then proceeds to place her spirit body into Anarcha's human body.

Anarcha is startled by the invasion of age, as well as, Olive is bewildered by the youthful life infused with morphine by Anarcha. Olive stands inside of Anarcha's stupor and stumbles, and then steadies herself with a new fond purpose. Olive inside Anarcha's body holds on to items in the building and walks toward each woman's station. After a minute of un-equilibrium, Olive/Anarcha find a glass beaker and sees her reflection with Olive standing inside her. It is confusing to both of them. They walk gingerly over to the medication table and both grab the morphine/opium jar making certain she took the correct pills.

The moaning of the women catches their attention and they stumble toward the other women. Olive/Anarcha begins to clean the women, washing their bodies and cleaning them up quickly and efficiently. Some of the women are combative and are psychologically violated with anyone touching them and are reluctant for help. Anarcha is the more dominant one. Olive is emerging out of the stupor is able to hum a songful melody that is able to calm the women. When she slows her soulful rendition, the women's psychosis erupts again. Anarcha/Olive continue bathing the women, washing hair, massaging and genuine comforting each other as humming a melody of sisterly and motherly's love.

Through the session, as Anarcha/Olive pass a patient, she reaches out, grabs them and pulls them toward her.

OLDER/YOUNG WOMAN

Thank you

The older/young looks into the eyes of two people, but not certain what to make of it. Her eyes again adjust at the sight of two spirits mixed but Anarcha/Olive are more captured by the fixation of the woman's stare.

OLDER/YOUNG WOMAN (CONT'D)

Take my breath!

Stunned by the thought, Anarcha/Olive dart in both directions, which causes their bodies to drop completely to the floor. They stand again eyeing the woman who remains deadpan looking upward and through them.

OLDER/YOUNG WOMAN (CONT'D)

River me home!

Olive wants to speak, but Anarcha is mute but only able to hum. Their eyes searching the entire room, frantically considering what they been asked to do.

Olive waves Anarcha hands frantically no, Anarcha joins in attempting to pick-up the humming to a happier song.

The older/younger woman grip their hands and places it on her abdominal baby bump. Both Anarcha/Olive jump back at the suggestion that a child is present. The victim's tears trickle down her face. Her bloodshot eyes are penetrating Anarcha and Olive's hearts.

OLDER/YOUNG WOMAN (CONT'D)

Take my breath! Please!

EXT. TRAINS, BOATS AND BUGGYS TRAVELING

There is a montage of shots depicting Dr. Coop traveling to
Europe, Boston, Philadelphia, Washington D.C., North Carolina. He is seen signing books and speaking to large segments of the medical population. He is also applauded by large crowds and series of checks and cash are given to him. Dr. Coop's travels are done by steamships, as well as locomotives. Coop's final destination is New York City.

INT. NEW YORK: DAY-LARGE HOTEL- INSIDE A LARGE AUDITORIUM

Dr. Coop picture is depicted behind a podium, along with a sign naming him the father of Gynecological Services of America. There is a spectacular round of applause and the audience of respected dignitaries stand in reverence to Dr. Coop. On both sides of the podium are scientific men as Dr. Coop and is about to speak. The host of the event speaks first.

HOST

Thank you, fellow doctors! It is with great honor that we welcome and
celebrate a researcher, innovator, physician-extraordinaire in the area of

women's studies. Now with the funding available made to us by the successes of Dr. Coop, we can now open the first Women's health Center in New York City. Without further ado, please welcome Dr. Coop for your questions.

Dr. Coop rises from his seat, dressed in a traditional tux, shakes the hand of the host and stands behind the podium to the sounds of cheers, and applause. He waves at his colleagues in appreciation and motions for them to be seated.

DOCTOR COOP

Thank you, fellow physicians. It is with great pleasure that I thank you for this great reward of allowing me to open this great hospital to service the women of New York, dedicated to all research involving the gynecological present, past and future surgeries. I am also pleased that I am in New York because of the innovative medical services, but it is also the last stages of my trip. Glad to be back in the United States. It certainly will be great to return to South Carolina and my bed.

The host interrupts and walks to the podium, addresses the audience as well as Dr. Coop.

HOST

Yes, the floor is now open. Dr. Coop will take questions.

There are murmurs from the crowd and a young medical student emerges and approaches the microphone. All eyes are on her because of her approaching status as a female medical student in a predominately male profession.

FEMALE MEDICAL STUDENT

Good Morning Dr. Coop. Although, I am a woman, what are your thoughts on females in the South becoming medical doctors similar to the limited opportunities in the North?

Dr. Coop is uncomfortable with the question, glances at his host for assurance. The host asserts himself toward the microphone and speaks.

HOST

Thank you for the question young lady, however, as a rule we limit our questions to inquiries that are medical related.

The host begins scanning the audience for other hands which are male in nature. The host points to another hand but the female medical student interjects.

FEMALE MEDICAL STUDENT

Excuse me, I do have a medical related question for our guest at our institution specifically geared towards women.

Slightly embarrassed publicly, the host yields to the female medical student again.

FEMALE MEDICAL STUDENT (CONT'D)

Dr. Coop, I've read all of your work and it seems you've done tremendous work on female subjects in order to close the opening that so many women have after childbirth.

The female medical student pulls out a copy of Dr. Coop's published work and holds it up high and continues.

FEMALE MEDICAL STUDENT (CONT'D)

The information in here mentions the number of women from your research, which is quite fantastic. How were you able to get the consent of the white women and their husband's permission to use a scalpel, suture, repair multiple disorders and arrive where we are right now?

Coop apprehensively laughs at the question, approaches the audience and the microphone, while fumbling with it nervously.

DOCTOR COOP

Young lady, young lady, let us give this little philly a round of applause at her boldness at speaking at such a male dominated medical school.

The audience lightly applauds.

DOCTOR COOP (CONT'D)

Yes, there were quite a few women who help significantly with the research and they were quite taken care of during the trials. The women were housed and fed. The facilities were pristine and no harm were done to them. Believe me they were quite comfortable.

The female medical student points to Dr. Coop's published work and at Dr. Coop in a threatening manner.

FEMALE MEDICAL STUDENT

In light of the economic and convenience of slavery for medicine in South Carolina, are you suggesting that all of your female experiments were white?

DOCTOR COOP

Yes, we do have slaves and property on my land, and some of the slaves
were on hand to assist in the procedures. However, no harm came to any
white women under my care and experiments. Thank you.

There is a large applause from the audience of male doctors as the female medical tries to offer a rebuttal but is
sounded out and males stepping around her to pose more questions to Dr. Coop. He acknowledges the applause
and leans back and whispers to his Host.

DOCTOR COOP (CONT'D)

Who was that abolitionist?

HOST

I believe she goes by the name of Blackwell.

INT. BARN BUILDING

Olive/Anarcha slowly backs away from the older/young pregnant woman. Her body shaking no. The woman's
eyes plead for her to come back. Olive/Anarcha backs into a brass pan, turns around and sees her reflection.
Olive also emerges from the reflection. Both sets of eyes flutter back and forth. Anarcha takes control, shakes
her head violent and looks at the ground. They both approach the sickly woman. They stop and dart toward the
medicine table. Anarcha quickly pours a multiple of different types of pills and begins crushing them and adding
different liquids to the concoction. Olive inside of her tries to force her to speak aloud. Anarcha opens her
mouth but nothing comes out. Anarcha, takes both her hands and squeezes her mouth shut. Anarcha takes the
concoction in the liquefied form in the jar walks toward the sick woman.

Anarcha's walks are labored. Olive is fighting to remain still. The walk is lumbered and difficult with the internal
flesh verses spirit fighting for supremacy. Anarcha raises the head of the woman to help her drink. The woman
is anxiously waiting for the liquid. The woman's white dry lips moisten as she swallows the deadly potion.
Anarcha lays the woman's head down from the forty-five degrees. Olive, through one eye of Anarcha, has tears
flow, while the Anarcha's other eye is saturated with anger and revenge.

The older/young pregnant lies back, roughly grabs her abdomen and her throat. She then grabs the side of the
bed with her wrist shaking the sides of the bed indicating the deadly pain bolts is slashing her insides.
Olive/Anarcha backs-up as the woman shouts and screams. Behind Olive/Anarcha, the other women raise
themselves in various comfortable positions and watch intently at the agony of a labored death of a mother and
child.

There is silence. Olive/Anarcha walks over and sees the woman fixed pupils looking at her. Anarcha eyes are
ignoring compassion, while viewing the body sinisterly, as Olive's eyes continues to weep. Anarcha turns her
dejected self and looks at the other women sitting intently watching her. One by one in silence each cup their
hands and with Olive/Anarcha fighting to walk toward and against the women's bedside. Anarcha's flesh gives
the women each a drink from the mixing bowl and then lay back silently with their eyes fixed skyward. Olive's
spirit is continually fighting for superiority, falling to the filthy floor trying to detach herself from the flesh of

Anarcha. After all the women have drunk from the bowl, Anarcha closes their eyes with their hands, then quietly goes over to her cot and scans the room for survivors and places the bowl on the table.

Olive is completely dejected and depressed but Anarcha's flesh pushes on. She crawls to the medication table and begins making another concoction. Olive looks around at the deceased women and ponders what else can Anarcha do? Anarcha/Olive leans on the table with the bowl in her hand, then proceeds to swallow the contents. Olive is flabbergasted and tries to flee from inside Anarcha, but she remains steadfast inside her flesh. Anarcha/Olive stumble together and fall on to the floor. Both of their eyes are looking in different directions trying to find stability. Anarcha begins smiling, while Olive eyes begins to tear as the battle continues. Anarcha/Olive begin crawling across the blood-soaked floor. Out of the corner of Olive's eye, she sees an unhinged nail protruding from the floor. Olive/Anarcha spirit pushes the body more and more, while the flesh desires to lay dormant. With a heave and deep breath Olive/Anarcha exerts Anarcha's body to the nail and falls face first on to the wooden floor. Olive feels the shadow of death blanketing Anarcha as her breath slows. Olive out of breath from pushing against the flesh looks heavenly, and with a thrust of spiritual strength she lunges Anarcha body forward and attaches her clothing to the nail. Anarcha is out cold from the face-fall and Olive again pushes and yanks herself out of Anarcha's body as the spirit of death shadows Anarcha body. Olive extremely exhausted, falls a few feet away from Anarcha to rest.

EXT. STREETS OF NYC-DAY

The host and Coop are walking the streets and he is showing him the sights of the vibrant city. The host is pointing out various attractions and, in a distance, the host motions for Coop to follow him into a large tent.

I/E. LARGE TENT SAME TIME

Inside the tent there is a band playing festive music and there are animals and clowns and all of the trimmings of a festival atmosphere. The host guides Coop across a floor of rock gravel mixture to the front of the seats and Coop is reluctant to sit but the host urges him into the seat.

> HOST
> It's okay. I had these reserved for us. I know the owner.

Coop and the host sit and begin to enjoy the big-top show. The Master of Ceremony, a man with a tall hat, comes from behind a curtain with a microphone and gets the audience of people who have accumulated behind the host and Coop into an excited frenzy. In between pumping up the crowd, he waves at the host, who acknowledges his presence.

Also, free food and peanuts are distributed to the host and Coop. T. C. ARNUM the master of ceremony speaks.

T. C. ARNUM

Great evening ladies and gentlemen! We have set aside a great moment
in our show, that will allow everyone in the event to become a part of
the show. How does that sound?

There is a roar from the crowd and a load applause. The host and Coop sit up in their seats eager to listen.

T. C. ARNUM (CONT'D)

Okay everyone, look at the ground below your feet. Now stomp on
it real loud and make some noise!

The audience does as directed, and the sound of stopping feet is heard which sounds like thunder inside the tent.

T. C. ARNUM (CONT'D)

Okay everybody, reach down and pick up a bunch of rocks and stones in
both hands and hold them until I say we can play! Now everyone repeat
after me!

There is a pause as the audience holds the rocks and stones in their hands pounding the floor with their feet with anticipation.

Music is playing loudly as the audience gets louder and louder. T.C Arnum motions for two of his stage hands from behind a curtain. The stage-hands wheel out a six-foot platform covered at the top, two more men come from behind the curtain to the main event. Each has a whip in his hands and stands on each corner of the platform facing the platform. One hands T.C. a pull string and T.C., turns and faces the crowd, who has raised their excitement to a frenzy. T. C. shouts to the crowd, first starting slow then builds up.

T. C. ARNUM (CONT'D)

Hit a nigger, hit a nigger, hit a nigger.

With lightning speed T.C., snatches the cover off the platform and on top of the platform are two black men whose head and arms are in a stockade contraption. Each are able to move from side to side, but if they attempt to disembark from the platform they are whipped by the stages-hands below them. T.C. Arnum encourages the audience to continue throwing the stones and rocks at the men on the platform, while music plays, laughter and amusement entertains the audience.

Some of the audience hit the black men as if they were a bullseye and the crowd roars with laughter. Audience members are awarded different souvenirs for hitting the targets. Coop and host participate but miss their targets. While the event continues, T. C. beckons for the host and Coop to follow him outside the tent.

EXT. OUTSIDE OF THE TENT MOMENTS LATER

The three men standing within ear shot of the event and sounds, T.C., continually looks back over his shoulder at the tent, but wants to make light conversation.

> HOST
>
> T.C. Arnum, please allow me to introduce you to a prominent physician
> who is visiting our great city for the first time. This is Dr. Wolfgang Coop.

The two gentlemen shake hands and exchange smiles.

> DOCTOR COOP
>
> Great show sir, great show! Will your show be traveling to the great
> southern state of South Carolina? T.C., smiles greatly at that statement.

> T. C. ARNUM
>
> If there is money to be made, I'll be there!

The roar of crowd diverts T.C.'s attention. He becomes more anxious, pacing back and forth and fidgeting with his loose change in his pockets.

> T. C. ARNUM (CONT'D)
>
> Look gentlemen, I do appreciate you coming but I do have to get back
> to the show.

He attempts to walk off, but pauses and looks at Coop as an afterthought.

> T. C. ARNUM (CONT'D)
>
> You say you're a physician, right?

Coop nods his head and host speaks up.

> HOST
>
> The best male doctor for any female in the country.

T. C., looks at the host sarcastically.

> T. C. ARNUM
>
> Then you might want to come to my event in a week. A lot a medical
> people will be there and I can make a least 1,000 dollars.

Both host and Coop are surprised at the number as T. C., walks away. Coop taps at his shoulder, T.C., glances back.

DOCTOR COOP

How can we help or become a part of this event?

T. C. ARNUM

You can't but you can invest in the event by coming to the showcase.

T.C. Arnum reaches into his jacket and pulls out a flyer and tosses it to host who catches and opens it up and shows Coop. The flyer mentions a public dissection of a slave woman who claimed to be the mammie of the first president of the United
States, who happened to be the oldest living human being. Just as T.C., is about to enter the tent, Coop shouts back to T.C.

DOCTOR COOP

Can you make this kind of money with a dissection?

T.C. responds.

T. C. ARNUM

You could always earn money off niggers, dead or alive. Hope to see you
there.

Host and Coop follow T.C., toward the tent but are blocked at the tent by two burley brutes, and one motions toward the ticket counter. They both look toward T.C., who looks back at them with a coy smile and holds his hands in a cavalier manner. Host and Coop shrug and turn and depart, Coop shoves the flyer in his inside jacket.

INT/EXT: BARN BUILDING DAYS LATER

Coop arrives at the door of his barn dressed and ready for work. He immediately pauses because Anarcha has not opened the door as she normally does. He forces the door and enters.

INT: BARN BUILDING MOMENTS LATER

Once inside, the silence is breath-taking, with his keys Coop opens a gun closet near the entrance and removes a loaded double barrel shotgun. He moves around the room lighting lanterns and once noticing the room is safe from intruders continues to survey the room. He then begins to check the pulse of each patient and becomes frantic with the results of each patient is dead. Coop begins turning tables and chairs over at the thought of all his subjects have been killed. He begins turning over the cots with the women inside as their lifeless bodies drop to the floor. He stops for a second and begins counting the women and finds that one is missing. He frantically, begins picking up items, uncovering things, searching through the victims' bodies. Coop shouts out!

DOCTOR COOP

Anarcha! Anarcha! Anarcha!

There is still no sound. Then he falls on some debris and finds her. He checks her pulse and it is faint. Olive awakens and silently moves away from Coop and Anarcha. Coop falls down and holds Anarcha in his arms, almost crying at the thought of losing her. After a moment, he gathers himself and tries to awaken her. Anarcha does not respond. He goes to gather water from a bucket and throws the water in her face. The shock of the water awakens Anarcha as she coughs and gags. She is awake and looking at her master ashamed. Coop shouts at her.

DOCTOR COOP (CONT'D)

What happen! Who destroyed my lab and killed my patients? Was it
those Yankees or those runaway slaves? What about those jealous
doctors of private practice? Tell me.

Coop violent shakes Anarcha to no avail. She opens her mouth and he ceases shaking her because of her missing tongue. Frustrated, he plops down on a chair he toppled over earlier in his rampage. Coop just sits still looking at Anarcha. Olive appears staring and wondering what will transpire. Anarcha gains her faculties and stands. She looks at Coop who is still stoic but watches her. She begins to clean up the lab, picking up items and turn the cots over and placing the women on the cot although they are dead. Coop jumps up and rummages through items spilled on the floor and finds a Morse code machine, and then starts tapping out a message. Anarcha comes near him and he motions for her to move away from him. He stomps his feet and points for Anarcha to go in a different direction. When she walks in a right direction, he pounds the butt of his shot-gun on the floor indicating she is right where he wants her to be.

In a few moments, the Morse code machine begins sending back a message as Coop begins to transpire the message. He writes down the wording and he pounds the butt of his shotgun on the wooden floor as Anarcha stands over a floor basement door. Coop takes a key out of his pocket in between transpiring a message and tosses it in Anarcha's direction. She reluctantly picks up the key and shakes her head no in Coop's direction.

DOCTOR COOP (CONT'D)

Open it! Open it now!

With minimal strength, Anarcha opens the basement floor-door and stands at the edge looking back at Coop. Olive proceeds to walk toward the opening. Coop shouts at Anarcha, which makes Olive shutter and look back at him.

DOCTOR COOP (CONT'D)

Get me some barrels, plenty of them.

Anarcha grabs a lantern and descends the stairs. Olive approaches the opening and looks into the dimly lit dungeon but cannot see anything. The audible sound of Anarcha coming up the stairs with a large barrel to the edge of the opening and rolling toward Coop. Coop moves closer to the edge of the opening and as soon as Anarcha brings them to the edge of the opening and rolls them out he stands them up. It is exhausting work for Anarcha. She does all of the heavy lifting up the stairs to the platform. Olive just stands there. Each time she attempts to venture into the darkness, another large whiskey barrel is brought upward. Anarcha is sweating and breathing hard. When the last one is brought up and set right side up, Coop sits down in a chair. His shotgun still in his hand with the butt of the weapon on the floor.

DOCTOR COOP (CONT'D)

Get me a drink!

Anarcha scrambles out of the floor basement, slams the door, rummages through the debris of items on the floor and locates a whiskey bottle. Anarcha also finds a shot glass. She glances back a Coop who is taking off the lids of the barrels one by one. Anarcha turns her back to Coop, brings empty the shot-glass to mouth and takes a deep breath. She then unloads a wad of mucus and saliva combined silently in the shot-glass. She then pours the whiskey in the glances stirs it with a finger and turns to bring it to Coop. Coop is continual opening all lids of the barrels. He grabs the glass and Anarcha backs up. Olive chuckles to herself and moves away from floor basement. Coop then proceeds to sit in a chair with the shot-gun across his thigh pointing in Anarcha's direction.

DOCTOR COOP (CONT'D)

I need you to finish taking the lids off the barrels.

Anarcha does as she told to do. She completes the task in no time. Coop also yanks out a piece a paper and hands it to Anarcha.

DOCTOR COOP (CONT'D)

Write it exactly the way it is in written.

Coop motions for Anarcha to go and gather paint and brush items in a corner. Coop points out the exact letters as they are written on the paper. Anarcha, barrel by barrel, duplicates the letters from the design given by Coop. The initials are all written in white against the brown backdrop barrels. Anarcha writes slowly as a new learner but inscribes the following letters HU, UGA, MCG, DU, BU, UVA, YU, UA, UT, and UM Med schools. Coop holds the glass the entire time. As Anarcha finishes the last of the letters, he swallows all of the liquid in on shot, and wipes his brow.

DOCTOR COOP (CONT'D)

Now, put their bodies in the barrels!

At first Anarcha is confused at what she just heard. She holds her hand over her ear suggesting to Coop that she has not completely heard what he asked of her.

DOCTOR COOP (CONT'D)

You heard me the first-time girl. Put the bodies in the barrels.

Exhausted from bringing up the barrels from the floor basement, Anarcha, one by one, places the former patients of Coop in to the large whiskey barrels. Some of the women's dead weight fatigues her and she has to leverage each on her shoulder. Coop walks around her surveying her work and as she stuffs the bodies into the barrels some of the extremities protrude out. Coop begins pouring bottles of whiskey in the barrels filling the barrels to the brims. Once all of the women have been placed in the barrels, Coop motions for Anarcha to pick up the lids. She picks up the lids and then Coop motions for her to place the lid on the barrel despite the extremity. Coop, from behind his back reveals a hack saw and proceeds to surgically sever the extremities of the women's arms, legs, fingers or any body parts that impedes the progress of forcing the lid on. The blood and excess body parts fall to the floor and Anarcha gags at the sight of the carnage. Olive stands back in shock at such a sight.

After several minutes, all of the lids are closed and shut. The blood and whiskey permeate the floor near where they are standing. Coop hands Anarcha a bag and motions for Anarcha to pick up the body parts into the bag. She does so and is still gaging at the request. Anarcha moves away from Coop. She stands adjacent to one empty barrel with the letters MCG marked on it. Anarcha begins looking around the floor and the lab for perhaps another body. Coop sits again with the shotgun aimed at Anarcha.

DOCTOR COOP (CONT'D)

You the only one that could have done it! I know it was you! You
pushed my research back ten years. No one else comes here. For the
first time I wish you could talk and tell me why!

Anarcha is frighten but a little relieved that her secret has been found out. Olive is standing between them and she slowly backs up. Olive becomes more frighten for Anarcha. Olive looks around for something to help Anarcha. There is nothing. Anarcha stands and begins humming, nothing significant but the same song that she hummed to soothe the other women when she was soothing them initially. With her hands extended upward and her head downward, she closes her eyes and looks heaven bond. Then looks at Coop and smiles. Coop pulls both triggers on the shotgun which lifts Anarcha's body at least two feet into the air splattering her entire chest wall across different parts of the barn. The hole in her back cavity disintegrates from bone and tissue to cell specimen samples. As the rest of body descends, it falls right on top of the empty barrel marked MCG. Coop then proceeds to place the rest of her mutilated body into the barrel with inflicting any additional harm on the deceased.

INT. TALIFFARIO BUILDING MCG OFFICE

Inside are one white doctor and he is looking out a window watching a slave auction. Several other white doctors are sitting at a long table. The doctor, ONE PHYSICIAN, at the window speaks first.

ONE PHYSICIAN

Gentlemen, thank you all for being so prompt. It seems that the challenge we have as medical schools across the country is that of retaining our own red blood Southern American boys for out next generation of physicians.

There is an agreement amongst the members at the table. Physician One comes and sits at the table and he tosses two hundred dollars on the table. The others begin to toss in additional money on the table.

THIRD PHYSICIAN

Now that we have an investment to make a decision, how do we proceed?

There is a silence, and one physician rises to speak while the others listen attentively.

ONE PHYSICIAN

What we need is recruitment. Recruiting members of our community to stay home and get a decent southern medical education and forget about the dam, Yankee medical schools.

FOURTH PHYSICIAN

Recruiting students shouldn't be a problem. It's just retaining them with the best resources.

Another physician throws in another hundred dollars into the kitty.

THIRD PHYSICIAN

I'm not certain I follow how this conversation is going.

One physician, walks back over to the window and again stares at the slave auction.

ONE PHYSICIAN

Right now, I need you to count the money on the table and go down stairs.

The Third Physician begins counting the money, slowly and methodically, then leaves the room. He is outside by the auction block. The Third Physician continually looks up toward the window and at the auction block.

EXT: SLAVE AUCTION BLOCK, TALIFFARIO BUILDING MCG OFFICE

There are several male and female slaves at the auction block, most are partially nude.

There are also field animals being auctioned off. They are being examined by various white men and women all over their entire bodies. An auctioneer is shouting out various prices that isn't audible to understand. Buyers are in the audience and are bidding. The winning bidders are paying the auctioneer and leaving with their slaves and animals.

A large slave is currently being auctioned. He is a prime specimen and the bids are coming in rapidly. Third Physician looks up at the window and his colleagues peer down at him not offering any advice. The slave is sold and others similar to him are also auctioned off. Children and mothers are separated and sold off. The auction is satisfactory and the amount of available slaves dwindles down. Third physician still awaits a signal from his investors.

INT. TALIFFARIO BUILDING MCG OFFICE

SECOND PHYSICIAN

I'm not certain why we are investing our money in a slave. Should we like the good doctor said be investing in retaining students to remain in the south?

The other physician looks at One Physician for answers. He looks at them and out the window. The he motions for all of them to come to the large window. They each assemble looking out the window down at the auction and Third Physician is flustered at how to proceed.

ONE PHYSICIAN

Gentlemen, the only way we can retain students is to purchase a slave, train him to do the things, we cannot or won't do because of the illegality, moral and code of our Socratic Oath.

FOURTH PHYSICIAN

What are you suggesting doctor?

ONE PHYSICIAN

In order to retain and recruit strong medical students and keep them to advance the medical community within the south, we need without question is cadavers! We need a highly trained slave to do what needs to be down which will take less strain off of us and help advance medical science.

As the physicians continually look at the auctions, One Physician looks in a distance into a field a few blocks from the auction block. He sees a slave tilling the land with an ox in his hand alone, as the sun begins to heat up. The slave is working diligently. One physician motions for his colleagues to look in the direction of the field hand. They do and agree with their eyes while frantically wave down to Third Physician to walk toward the field. He figures it out to leave the auction block and go into the field.

EXT. OPEN SEMI-PLOWED FEILD- MOMENT LATER

Third Physician is having a difficult time walking in the field with his nice shoes. He walks past the male slave and walks toward the large house in a distance. Third Physician continually walking and stepping in mud and dirt which is destroying his shoes. He spends a few minutes in the house and then an older white man emerges from the house counting cash money while standing on the porch. He shouts to the male slave, as Third Physician walks by.

> FARMER
>
> Boy! You his now! Go with your owner now!

The farmer goes back in the house still counting his newly found riches.

> THIRD PHYSICIAN
>
> Come on you. I have to get out of this dirt. You belong to MCG now.
> What name they call you? You can talk, can't you?

Third Physician looks back at the newly purchased slave. The newly purchased slave shakes his head at the thought of leaving and staying. He looks back and forth at the fields and the future and follows Third Physician.

> ZIPP
>
> I don't have a name sir. The master just never got around to it. He just
> told me to till the land and prepare for planting and harvest time.

Third physician paused in his pace looking straight ahead, then picks up his pace.

> THIRD PHYSICIAN
>
> Ok, ok, your new name is ZIPP, because you have to be quiet and learn
> a lot and not tell anybody who you work for. The name is Zipp, you got
> that?

> ZIPP
>
> Sir, thank you sir.

THERE ARE SERIES OF SHOTS AS ZIPP'S NEW EMPLOYERS MEET IN THE OFFICE BUIDING AND INSPECT HIM JUST LIKE THE AUCTION BLOCK, EXCEPT THEY DON'T EXAMINE HIS GENITALS.

FOURTH PHYSICIAN

I am glad he is not attractive, therefore, he won't have any of the
wenches coming around to see him.

Zipp is ashamed of the comment and continues to stand at attention.

SECOND PHYSICIAN

You are right, and also his significant physical stature is less threatening
and he can be easily be overcome if he ever gets out of hand.

Zipp takes a deep sigh and again is hit with the comment about his height and his physical appearance. One physician puts a chair between Zipp and the physicians. Everyone grabs a seat and they all stare at Zipp for several long seconds.

There is a montage of shots of each physician introducing themselves, tells their responsibility to MCG and what will transpire for the job he is about to do, including what he is expected to do and his title as a porter, that will be compensated.

ZIPP looks at each physician, as they watch him. There is still a hesitancy to look at them and he is surprised that they have asked if he had any questions of them. ZIPP opens his mouth and he whispers it out.

ZIPP

You doctors from MCG told me a lot of things I'm suppose to do because
I work for you. Yet, I heard it all, but one thing stood out, that I just want
to be clear that I heard. Did you doctors say you were going to pay me a
salary for my duties here?

All of the doctors chuckle and nod their heads in agreement. In unison, the doctors leave the room rubbing his head, except for Physician One. Physician One just stands there looking at ZIPP.

ONE PHYSICIAN

Get up out that chair. We have some learning to do!

ZIPP jumps up and is attentive to the Physician. The doctor goes to a closet and pulls a light-colored blue jacket. There is another white jacket also.

ONE PHYSICIAN (CONT'D)

When you get good one day, I'll let you wear the white one, maybe.

ZIPP becomes attentive at the thought!

ZIPP

Sir, are you saying one day I'll be a doctor, like you?

Physician One looks at ZIPP sarcastically.

> ONE PHYSICIAN
>
> Boy, you know well, there ain't no such thing as a coon doctor! You just
> follow what I say and I can make you a good assistant! I need to get you
> ready for the barrels. Stop talking and listen!

ZIPP snatches off his work clothes and neatly folds and places them on a stool. He takes pride in placing on the scrub blue jacket and follows Physician One around the room as he points out various jobs and tools.

There is a montage of shots of Physician One training ZIPP in the care of the lab and the anatomy of the human body. Physician One is also teaching ZIPP to read and write. There are also shots of Physician One explaining to ZIPP a lesson or a procedure that must be done in the lab. Physician One takes ZIPP into a massive lecture hall and shows him where physicians will speak to other physicians, standing at a lecture. ZIPP is amazed at the opportunity that is before him. Physician One then points to a side table and stool far off the center of the stage and assigns his desk there as an observer.

INT: BARN BUILDING NIGHTS LATER

Olive is still devastated. Coop has all the barrels sealed and continually rolls them over to the front door. Olive for the first time begins to investigate the house. Olive merges into each room searching for items that can help. She finally merges into a make shift outhouse that is adjacent to the barn. The stench from the outhouse makes her stumble and she catches herself against a wall. As Olive steadies herself, she feels a curtain and adjacent to the curtain she touches a covered-up mirror. Olive uncovers a small mirror. For the first time she shows signs of relief and she almost sits down on the commode, but catches herself. Olive stands on the commode, but first places her hand on the mirror. Then with ease, her hand enters the mirror without resistance. Olive stands on the commode, then the sink and prepares to step into the mirror. Simultaneously Olive hears the galloping of horses approaching the barn and it diverts her attention. She also hears men's voices.

Olive climbs down and opens the door of the bathroom, which leads through the back-barn door, which faces the front door of the barn. Olive walks to the front and sees a white man on a buggy and two male slaves taking Coop's barrels from the barn and placing them on the buggy very rapidly. The barrel with Anarcha's body is the last to be placed on the buggy. Olive darts back to the bathroom and climbs as she did before, but hesitates even more now. The white man jumps down from the driver's seat, enters Coops barn, and begins counting out several hundred dollars for the barrels then leaves. Coop counts the money and closes the door. The white driver, grabs the reins of the horse and snaps the reins to take off, just as Olive jumps aboard the buggy, and sits atop the barrel marked MCG.

EXT. SHIPPING DOCK- LATE EVENING

The buggy with the barrels pulls into the dock. There are other slaves and white overseers directing the slaves to remove other barrels off wagons and placing them on the dock. There are also slaves on ships that are continually removing barrels and replacing barrels. Olive follows the barrel with Anarcha's body in it. She sits atop the barrel and can survey the thousands of barrels with lettering for distances all across the country. She steps away for one second to get a better look, then looks back at Anarcha's barrel and it has been replaced by another barrel. She frantically, tries to search for the barrel but it remains missing. Olive then stoops down on her knees and enters different barrels with her spirit.

I/E. INSIDE THE BARREL MOMENTS LATER

Only Olive's face enters the barrel to observe, but the spirit of death inside the barrel growls at the sight of an intruder. Olive exits out quickly. Olive enters another barrel and this time the spirit of death snaps and spits at her and confront her face to face angrily. Olive sticks her head out from amongst the barrels and still searches for Anarcha's barrel. Olive jumps from barrel to barrel. Then enters another barrel and nothing happens, but Olive is able to hear a person's breath sounds and sees the person's body upside down asleep. Olive exits the barrel, when she hears the sound of a ships horn.

EXT. SHIPPING DOCK- MOMENTS LATER

The slave-hands are snatching all of the barrels and placing on a ship, Olive is confused on which direction to go. She looks up at the moon light sky, sees a reflection from the water, and sees the other side of a barrel that is facing her. It reads the MCG backwards and Olive realizes it is Anarcha's barrel and she climbs on board of the ship. The ship cast its confederate flag high into the night flowing waters.

MCG-LAB NIGHT-MONTHS LATER

All the barrels from the recent shipment are aligned in the hallway. OLIVE is laying crossed them, not sleeping but resting and listening for activity. In a distance, a door opening and closing startles her. Olive sits up and scans the room, which is not well lit. Footsteps are heard approaching her. Olive sits up, snatches her shoes, and places them on. Olive then keeps her hands on the top of the barrel as a placeholder. A well-lit lantern enters the room held by ZIPP. He is alone. ZIPP quickly gets to work, grabbing the barrels and side wheeling each to a better part of the room where there is more light. Olive walks alongside the barrels following the one that has ANARCHA in it. Once the barrels come to a rest. ZIPP grabs a straight-icepick and sharpener from his desk. He slowly sharpens the icepick and starts at the beginning of the row of barrels and jams the icepick into the side of barrel creating a small hole and he watches as the contents spill out on to the floor and down into a built-in drain on the floor. ZIPP then stoops down and places his hand under the stream of liquid and examining the pools of liquid. OLIVE watches attentively, waiting for Anarcha's barrel. She stands atop of the barrel looking at the other barrels being brutally stuck with the straight-icepick. When Zipp stoops down under Olive's barrel, he examines the flow of liquid, which reveals its contents of blood mixed with water. The blood is fresh and flowing freely, not intermittent.

Zipp grabs the barrel, wheels it over to his examination table, and uses an antique can-opener to open the lid. Olive holds her breath in shock as Zipp slowly pours the heavily blood-soaked liquid onto the floor. Olive steps backward as Zipp with one hand extracts the human remains of Anarcha's body from the barrel on to the table. Olive slumps to a dry spot on the floor but reluctantly watches what is about to transpire.

With the skills of a learned anatomist. Zipp is careful to preserve Anarcha's body and lays it out respectfully. Zipp removes her clothing and she is nude; he lays a cloth across her breast and vaginal area. Anarcha's body, because of the shotgun blast, reveals the middle portion of the torso is gone, including her parts of her back. Zipp reaches below the examination table and pulls a lever, which changes the design of examination table revealing series of holes in the table. Zipp then reaches into his side-holster and pulls out a well sharpen dagger. Zipp proceeds to cut Anarcha's skin off body, and places the different sections he has removed in to a bin. Olive is devastated, begins crying, and holds her head and upward. She screams in her tears but nothing can be heard. Olive turns her back as the sound of slicing flesh as if something is being butchered continued with the flesh being tossed in to a bin and the sound of dripping pools of blood descend from the table into a pan or spills onto the floor. The dripping is similar to light or heavy rain upon a roof.

Olive quickly spins around, as Zipp continues his dissection, labeling and note taking. Olive jumps up, runs over to the barrels, and begins reexamining each barrel quickly and efficiently. She can't move them, but highly reluctant to enter into the barrel as a spirit again because of the death spirit that inhabits the barrel. Olive remains on the outside and places her ear to the side of the barrel. She also checks the liquid spilling out. Zipp did not puncture all of them, only a few. Olive closes her eyes but every now and then glances back at Zipp cutting the flesh of Anarcha's body to make certain he is finished yet. Zipp is now removing the organs and categorizing each specimen. Olive again closes her eyes with her ears she listens attentively. She moves from barrel to barrel trying to listen.

INT. INSIDE THE BARREL MOMENTS LATER

Inside the barrel, the soft sound of a hibernating breathing is heard along with the rhythm of the heartbeat. Olive hears the breathing, and her spirit enters the barrel reluctantly, peaking inside the barrel barley enough to see a woman's body in major contortions and upside down in the barrel. She is asleep, but breathing. Olive exits the barrel and stands in the lab.

She slumps to the floor after the challenge, exhausted at the battle in the spiritual realm. Olive gazes in Zipp's direction, and jumps up and walks over and stands across from Zipp staring down at Anarcha's skeleton minus a few of the bones. Anarcha's body is absent of all flesh, organs removed and now Zipp is washing the bones with bleach attempting to remove the blood tinged color from the bone specimens. Anarcha's body is laid out in the anatomical position and with one yank, Zipp is able to lift and display lateral view of the skeleton without tearing or breaking any bones. On the side view, it reveals where the bones were shattered or missing from the shotgun blast. Olive looks up at Zipp who remains steadfast at his work and oblivious to Olive's spirit. Zipp lays the bones down leaves the table and goes to a room he has to unlock. Zipp takes a lantern, enters the room, and places the lantern on the wall.

INT. DIMLY LIT ROOM MOMENT LATER

Zipp is in the room and there is the sound of rattling and breaking. Olive hear the noises and walks toward the room and the light as she approaches a louder sound of breakage, snapping and cutting is heard. Just as she reaches the open door to enter, Zipp exits, jarring Olive that she speedily steps away before he walks through her. The lantern is in his hand and darkness remains in the room. Zipp turns back and closes and locks the door then returns to Anarcha's skeleton. Zipp then proceeds to replace Anarcha's missing ribs and skeleton pieces with the ones he has in his hands. He used an adhesive liquid to align the entire body attaching each skeletal bone to one another. Zipp then flips the skeleton back to the prone position and proceeds to stand at the head of the table with the skull under him. Underneath the table, he pulls out a curved icepick and immediately lightly thrust the icepick's sharpen end into the direct center of top of the skull. Zipp then goes to a closet, pulls out a stand with a large hook at the top and with a round bottom-base, and carries it over to the examination table. With care Zipp then lifts Anarcha's skeleton by the icepick and the rattling of the bones clinging together like bamboo wind chimes makes Olive cover her ears. Once attached onto the pole. Zipp takes the Anarcha's skeleton specimen to the front entrance of the lab on display admiring his work. Olive is on the floor crying profusely, in between tears and crying she gathers herself sits atop the barrel and listens to the sound of rhythmic breathing and heartbeat inside the barrel.

INT: MOMMENTS LATER IN THE LAB

Zipp is moving from each barrel again puncturing each barrel with the straight icepick and letting the blood and whiskey flow to the floor.

Olive is standing now on top of the barrel desperately trying to find a way to thwart Zipp's direction. There is none. Zipp moves so fast he jams the icepick in to Olive's barrel and keeps moving down the row of multiple barrels. The row of barrels is flowing to the drainage of whiskey and blood. Zipp looks down the rows and slowly walks backwards and whisk his gloved hand through each barrel's flow of liquid. He stops at Olive's barrel. Olive stoops down waiting for Zipp's reaction, at the zero flow of liquid. Zipp kneels and looks through the icepick opening to no avail. Zipp then grabs the barrel, as Olive jumps off. Zipp sideways rolls the barrel to the center of the room, grabs a hammer and chisel, and proceeds to open the lid of the barrel. Upon the opening of the lid, Zipp notices the body of a woman, who is upside down, he lifts the barrel with ease and places it on his examination table, then flips the barrel right side up. The body does not spill out. Zipp proceeds to shake the barrel and the body falls on to the table. The specimen as far as Zipp can see is in full tack, she is dressed modestly and he believes she is deceased. Zipp begins to undress the woman as he is about to disrobe her, he notices a breath and a sigh. Zipp takes a step back and collects himself, still surveying the circumstances. Zipp moves closer to the table, reaches under the table, pulls out a hand mirror, places it under the subject's nose and mouth for several seconds, and sees the breath and mist on the mirror. Zipp then places his head on her chest listening for breath sounds and listens for a heartbeat. While he is doing this, TANZY slowly awakens. She looks down at Zipp from the examination table.

                              TANZY
              That's no way to treat a lady!

Zipp jumps up, certainly surprised, and backs away from the table, just staring at Tanzy. Tanzy slowly sits up on her arm after her ordeal.

                         TANZY (CONT'D)

              Is this Philadelphia?

Zipp just nods his head in the negative and helps her sit to a forty-five-degree angle. Tanzy brings her legs and lets them dangle on the edge of the table. She also adjusts her skirt and clothing so not to reveal anything and maintaining her modesty.

TANZY (CONT'D)

How long have I been here? Who are you? Why are you dressed as if you are a doctor, ain't you a slave? Wait, Wait, did you say this is Philadelphia?

ZIPP

I didn't say anything ma'am.

Tanzy voice because a little raised.

TANZY

Say something! I need to know where I am and what I am doing here!

Zipp, stares at Tanzy and points his finger while he talks.

ZIPP

I know the lady needs to simmer down, because this is my lab and I'm not suppose to be keeping company and I'm suppose to be the only one here and this is my lab during the night. Therefore, it would be best if you simmer down your voice so not to bring attention to my bosses.

Zipp notices his finger pointing and subtly puts it away. Tanzy softens her voice and addresses Zipp.

TANZY

I am glad you put that finger away. That is no way to treat a lady, pointing a finger at her and talking to her in such a manner. Now can you please tell me where I am so I can hurry and leave!

Tanzy tries to stand but her legs are weak and wobbly, Zipp secures her waist and settles her back to the examination table. Tanzy places her arm on Zipp's shoulder for assurance. There is a significant height difference between Tanzy and Zipp.

Zipp holds up both his hands causing Tanzy to pause her conversation.

ZIPP

First miss lady, who fell out of a whiskey barrel, we have not been properly introduced. Second, I have work to do and I don't have the time to explain everything to you.

Tanzy, in frustration, takes a deep breath. Olive is in the background watching.

Olive comes over to the table and begins searching for something on the table that has been covered up by the sheets and blankets or place back into the lower cabinets below the examination table. She is too is also frustration at not knowing where to look.

Tanzy brushes her clothing and mashes down her shorthair. She looks in Zipp's direction, although, he has turned around and heading to work on the other barrels. Tanzy extends her hand in Zipp's direction but he ignores it. Zipp speaks to Tanzy as he walks away.

> ZIPP (CONT'D)
>
> A lady doesn't introduce herself to a man. A man has to be introduced to
> a lady.

> TANZY
>
> Who going to introduce you to me, we are the only two people down
> here, how could that possibly happen?

As Tanzy makes the statement, Zipp has rolled over a barrel and places the contents of another body onto another examination table. All the body fluids and whiskey splashing to the floor and odor permeating the room. Tanzy with newfound strength eases her legs across the table and attempts to leave the exam table. Tanzy wraps herself around the sheets and hides herself because she can't go anywhere, much less scream. Zipp takes off his works gloves and turns in Tanzy's direction.

> ZIPP
>
> We are not here alone, this a University with many people. They call me
> Zipp!

He extends his hand toward Tanzy, but she does not take the offer.

> ZIPP (CONT'D)
>
> What is your name?

Tanzy slowly uncovers her face and mouths something but it is inaudible? Again, she attempts.

> TANZY
>
> My name is . . . What is this place?

Zipp, chuckles, and understands her confusion.

> ZIPP
>
> Tell me your name and I'll explain.

Tanzy swallows hard, and attempts to tell Zipp her name.

TANZY

Tan-Tan, Tanzy!

ZIPP

This is not Philadelphia anymore Tanzy.

Tanzy manages a soft smile, but she is uneasy. Zipp notices the apprehension.

ZIPP (CONT'D)

I'm a porter down in the lab.

Tanzy gives an odd look then responds.

TANZY

There is a dead body on that table. There's blood all over the floor and
running out of them barrels. You have on doctor clothes and there ain't
no such thing as a Negro doctor. You an undertaker?

Zipp smiles and walks toward Tanzy to calm her fears, but she places her hand up for him to stop in his tracks.

TANZY (CONT'D)

I'm not finished yet!

Zipp looks at her firmly and responds! His hand and one finger held high.

ZIPP

Oh, yes you are! You are a visitor in my lab and an uninvited guest. I have
permission to be here. Do you? Why were you in the barrel?

The thought and questions humble Tanzy and she backs away from her inquiry.

TANZY

I'm afraid. I'm afraid of what will happen again.

Zipp looks at her apprehension and the tone of her conversation. He sits upon a stool and urges her to continue her story.

TANZY (CONT'D)

I know now this is not
Philadelphia. I got in the barrel going to be free from rural South
Carolina. I didn't want to be a master's wench or his bed warmer. I
didn't want my children sold no more. I was trying to get up north to
Philadelphia to get settled and then go looking for my babies.

Zipp is dejected, wondering what to say.

ZIPP Go on!

INT. FLASH-BACK: SLAVE QUARTERS SEVERAL YEARS AGO TEENAGE TANZY

A white slave owner is standing over Tanzy as she is delivering twins by a slave midwife. One by one, the children emerge. In and out of pain episodes and consciousness, Tanzy reaches for her children to hold them the white owner shakes his head no and takes them away, she glances at the twin's mulatto skin color, and then she hears the children cry in a distance as a horse and buggy pull away.

INT: MOMMENTS LATER IN THE LAB

TANZY

Seven children gone! Four I didn't get to hold, two I never seen and one I
just heard cry off in a horse and buggy.

Zipp rises to his feet, goes to his locker and pulls out a canteen and some biscuits wrapped in a napkin and hands it to Tanzy.

ZIPP

You have to be hungry, several hours in a barrel, upside down. I know
you have to be hungry.

Shyly, Tanzy takes the items and dives right into them, without a pause or a blink; she devours the biscuit and dribbles the canteen water on her clothing in a rush to quench her hunger and thirst pangs. Zipp also pulls out some molasses for the biscuits, but the biscuit is already gone.

ZIPP (CONT'D)

We're in Georgia!

Zipp's words freezes Tanzy's chewing and she looks at him!

Tanzy pulls her knees and sheet up to her chest and begins to whimper as she does so and item under the sheets is moved toward the edge of the bed.

Olive charges toward the bed as the item slips from underneath the sheets and careens to the hard-bloody floor. Olives arrives just in time to catch the item, dissolves through her hands and fingers, and smashes to the floor.

The sound of the catches Tanzy and Zipp's attention, Zipp picks up the item and unwraps it from the sheets and it reveals the shattered mirror. He just tosses the broken pieces into a trashcan. Olive remains dejected.

Tanzy places her hand on Zipp's shoulder he acknowledges the apology and faces her.

                    ZIPP (CONT'D)
        I have to get you out of here, at least get you close to Philadelphia.

Tanzy looks up astonished at the thought! She wraps herself in the sheets again, as Zipp, provides another sheet for her to cover herself again.

                    TANZY
        I can't go back in that whiskey barrel. I'll be coming back here like that
        body on the table. Is that a slave woman's body?

Tanzy points to the examination table.

                    TANZY (CONT'D)
        You still ain't been clear to what you doing down here. A porter does all
        kinds of jobs. I have never heard or seen a slave doing any work with
        dead bodies. I know an undertaker don't use the kind of tools around
        this room.

Tanzy scans the room, she gets up from the table and begins to investigate that she is in a lab and sees the primitive tools used for dissection.

                    ZIPP
        You, don't worry about my job. You worry about getting to Philadelphia.

To Tanzy's surprise, from under Zipp's smock, he pulls out a pocket watch and checks it. Zipp then looks at the window at the top of the ceiling. He begins to start cleaning up the lab as quickly as possible. Tanzy steps out of the way as does Olive who remains hidden but can observe all that goes on.

                    TANZY
        Can I . . .

Tanzy walks over to Zipp and again the height different is significant. Tanzy looks down and in an apologetic manner. Zipp interrupts her conversation, while he still works to sanitize the lab.

                    ZIPP
        Can you get back into the barrel, there is about to be a lecture in this lab
        and the only one that is suppose to be in here this morning is me, not you
        and me!

                    TANZY
        Is that the way you gonna treat a lady? Are you going to make me kill myself

again?

Zipp raises his hands to stop the long debate, as he survey's the lab for anything out of place. Everything looks in order. He looks at Tanzy and measures her height with his hand against a closet and she is too tall. She shrugs her shoulders. There are men's voices that can be heard in a distance but are getting louder as they come closer to the lab. Zipp snaps his finger, jets to the examination table and begins washing the body furiously from head to toe, front and back. Zipp then turns the body over and places her in an anatomical position. He quickly runs to a closet to snatch off his bloody smock and places on a blue jacket. He turns around and searches for Tanzy who has disappeared just as the lab door opens full of new prospective doctors and lead physicians.

Through a series of shots, a lead physician begins lecturing the student doctors on dissecting a human cadaver. After the brief lecture, each of the physicians simultaneous begins working on different parts of the human anatomy of the cadaver on the table.

Physician One leaves the room and he yields the room to Zipp who walks around the room speaking to each physician concerning what and how they are dissecting the human body. Sometimes he nods to them as they perform a procedure correctly, other times he takes a tool out of their hand without touching them and places the primitive tools back in their hands using the correct method. While Zipp is walking around with his hands behind his back speaking to the all-white physicians, he is also searching for where Tanzy might be hiding. He remains clueless. Olive sits atop the barrels remaining invisible observing the dissection of one woman she knew.

Physician One reenters the lab and the student disengage from the dissection, the scene reveals how the students have removed every vital organ and dismembered the cadaver. The cadaver has also revealed many sections of the body that also has been clamped and sewed in attempt to clean up the invasive procedures. Physician One shakes all the prospective physicians' hands as they exit the lab and some others public- ally acknowledge Zipp with a nod of appreciation for his knowledge and training methods. As they leave the room, some are not able to hold their stomach and proceed to vomit in the lab, and then exit the door. Physician One looks at Zipp and gives him genuine nod of approval as he also exits the lab.

ONE PHYSICIAN

Just medical jurisprudence, Zipp, just medical jurisprudence!

The lab has blood and body parts all surrounding the cadaver. Zipp makes certain he secures the door from anyone else entering. He grabs his smock and begins cleaning up and searching for Tanzy. There is an eerie silence as he whispers out her name but to no avail. In a picture-perfect distance to visualize the entire dissection, there is movement from underneath several burlap bags. Tanzy unravels, unwraps, and pulls her long legs out bags. She also pulls one bag from over her head, and has a sigh of relief.

As Tanzy stands to stretch her long-legs and arms, Zipp motions for her to freeze, they both freeze as the sound of footsteps are heard walking back toward the lab. Tanzy drops to the floor and begins placing back on the bags and head. Zipp helps her but she rejects his helps and points toward to front door to unlock it. Zipp stands at attention, brushing himself off and quietly unlocks the door but doesn't open it. The footsteps outside of the lab walkup into the door and open the letter slot at the bottom of the door and drop in a newspaper that drops to the floor near the splatter blood and water. Zipp quickly gets the paper and inserts it in his side pocket. The footsteps walk in the opposite direction and can no longer be heard. Zipp again quietly locks the door. Tanzy emerges from the burlap bags.

> TANZY
>
> I'm getting almost use to these bags, it's a little rough but comfortable.
> What are they?

> ZIPP
>
> They are body bags!

Tanzy immediately jumps out and away from the bags, continually, wipes herself off, and shutters at the thought she was hidden in body bags. She gags at the thought. She notices the newspaper in Zipp's pocket and reaches for it. Zipp allows her and she begins to examine it as she walks gingerly around the lab, remaining clear of the dissecting materials and tools. Zipp begins to clean up then walks over to Tanzy, reaches up, and turns the newspaper right side up.

> TANZY
>
> White folks taught you to read?

Zipp continues to clean and respond.

> ZIPP
>
> I need it for this job. They also taught me to clean and if you want to talk,
> you have to clean.

> TANZY
>
> I want to learn to read, can you teach me?

> ZIPP
>
> You are not going to be here that long, remember you in my lab, you came
> in a barrel on your way to Philadelphia! I could have lost my job if they
> found you. I'm not a field hand no more. I ain't going back!

> TANZY
>
> You killing people! That's what it says in the Bible! You not suppose to kill!

> ZIPP
>
> How do you know what is says in the Bible? You a slave woman. You
> don't know how to read! You just had babies for your master!

> TANZY
>
> So, teach me! Plus, I heard preachers talk about the Bible. So, teach me!

> ZIPP

I have to clean this place, you going to Philadelphia I have to getting ready for more work.

> TANZY

If I can learn to read before I get to Philadelphia, it will be easier to read where I'm going. Then I can get myself settled as an upright lady. So, teach me to read Zipp!

Zipp walks over to a bookshelf and pulls out an older Bible and turns to a passage of scripture of 2 Corinthians 3:10 and reads aloud.

> ZIPP

"If a man does not work, he shall not eat"

Zipp takes back the newspaper and hands Tanzy the Bible. He inserts the newspaper back in his pocket.

> TANZY

What does that mean? I'm not a man. I lost my appetite watching what I saw in this room.

Zipp shakes his head.

> ZIPP

If you want me to teach you how to read, you have to clean with me. You were a slave. You know if a slave doesn't work or clean, what is he or she?

Realization comes over Tanzy and she puts the bible down and grabs a mop, she softly responds

> TANZY

A dead slave.

There are moments of silence as they both work through the room cleaning, Zipp does the difficult work of cleaning and disposing of the flesh and placing it in designated receptacles. Tanzy mops the blood and washes the floor with the mop and washes the sheets with an inside washboard.

> TANZY (CONT'D)

If you have all those books on the shelf and the bible, why are you reading the newspapers?

> ZIPP

Once you learn to read, you should read all you can. You learn to teach yourself not depend on a slave- owner to teach you or anybody else. It's called self-taught. The newspaper is just for my night work.

Tanzy looks at Zipp oddly, she attempts to say something but he turns his back to her and continues his work. Olive is disturbed at Zipp's statement and looks toward the locked floor door, contemplatively.

INT. ZIPP'S SHACK RIGHT BEHIND THE LAB.

On the outside of the shack, it looks dilapidated, upon entering it is quite unusual. Zipp enters the one room shack followed by Tanzy and Olive who enters through the walls as she pleases. The room is quite clean for a male porter at that time. Everything has its place. Zipp points out his bookshelves, which are full of books, he has learned and memorized. Zipp has made himself a desk and there are writing instruments, as well as, writing paper. There is also a cot that is made up of straw and it's sturdy. There is a curtain that covers up Zipp's shoes, suits and a vase with multiple colored flowers that are strategically placed in all of Zipp's suit lapels. Tanzy and Olive are impressed.

> TANZY
>
> How did you get all these clothes? A white man gave it to you?

She fingers the suits and ties and tries on the shoes which, but her feet are too big for his sizes. Zipp lightly brushes her hand away from the material. Zipp is miffed at the slight.

> ZIPP
>
> I earned the money to purchase these tailor-made custom suits. Everything in here I paid for.

> TANZY
>
> Those doctors pay you money to do what you do?

> TANZY (CONT'D)
>
> How come they pay you and don't pay slaves for the work they do in the fields, kitchen, mill and having their babies?

The question freezes Zipp.

> ZIPP
>
> Some these shoes and suits I have to wear, because some of those white folks at MCG, put me in some pictures and they all looking good, so they fix me up so I can fix myself up. If I don't fix myself up, who else is going to do it? Look, this is a one-room place, you can stay here for a little piece, but not long because I like things the way I like things just like my lab.

Zipp immediately reaches underneath his cot and pulls out a string and a blanket. He hammers a nail into the wall with the string attached to both ends into corners of the room. Zipp then throws the blanket over the string separating the Tanzy from Zipp. Zipp is near to the door, Tanzy is nearest to the wall, he also has maneuvered his only cot to her side and he creates a multiple blanket palate for himself.

> ZIPP (CONT'D)
>
> If you wake up in the middle of the night and I'm not here, don't be frighten. I'll return by first light.

There is no response, on the other side of the blanket. Tanzy is asleep, with a slight snore. Zipp goes over, sits at his desk and pulls out his paper. He takes a particular section out of the paper, reads it and circle items then places it under some books on the desk. Above Zipp's desk is a makeshift calendar, which reads the first day of September 15th and Zipp places a large x in the box. Olive continues to watch carefully.

THERE ARE A MONTAGE OF SHOTS INSIDE THE ZIPP'S SHACK OF TANZY AND ZIPP SLEEPING. SHE KEEPS THE ONE ROOM SHACK AS CLEAN AS POSSIBLE AND MAKING MEALS WHICH OFTEN SURPRISES ZIPP' ALTHOUGH HE IS NOT REQUIRING HER TO DO IT, HE IS GREATLY APPRECIATIVE. THERE ARE ALSO SHOTS OF ZIPP LEAVING ABOUT 3 AM AND NOT RETURNING UNTIL DAWN. ONE NIGHT BEFORE DUSK, THEY ARE LAYING ON THEIR SEPARTE SIDES OF THE ROOM.

> TANZY
>
> Where do you go after I fall asleep?

> ZIPP
>
> I don't go just when you fall asleep, I told you sometime I have to work nights.

> TANZY
>
> Then can I go with you some nights, sometimes I don't like being alone and I'm awake and I wondering where you may be going and then when you're coming back.

Zipp quickly sits up from his palate his feet on the floor. Just as he glances at the blanket to respond he does a double take because Tanzy standing at the edge of the curtain. She walks over and he helps her sit down next to him, the edge of their knees lightly touching. Zipp looks straight ahead, Tanzy looks at him sensual and touches the side of his face.

> TANZY (CONT'D)
>
> I've been wondering, that maybe you have a wife or a girlfriend you visit

on a plantation. Somebody with fancy clothes and shoes who talk like
white folk with doctors, you should have all the girls.

Zipp slightly looks up at Tanzy, their eyes meet. There is chemistry, both resist it. Zipp looks forward and downward again, avoiding eye contact.

> TANZY (CONT'D)
>
> I know a way I can thank you for rescuing me from the barrel, letting
> me live and feeding me and I can make it so you won't have to leave.

Zipp immediate stands and starts pacing the room. Tanzy stands and when Zipp paces back toward her, she stands in front of him.

Zipp takes her forearm and hand, leads her to her side of the room, and guides her the cot opens the covers and places her inside. Tanzy prepares for him to join her by opening up the blanket. Zipp backs away. Tanzy is bewildered.

> ZIPP
>
> I have a job to do at night. You are a lady. You don't have to give yourself
> away. You did that to the master and he sold your babies. When you
> think like that, you got poison inside. You ain't done healing!

Tanzy's tears trickle down her face, as Zipp walks to the other side of the curtain. Olive is sitting on the floor watching it all and semi-impressed.

> TANZY
>
> No man ever turned me down, I'm beautiful and they all wanted me.

> ZIPP
>
> Being brave is much more beautiful. Brave enough to know you have to
> get your healing done. Get some sleep.

The room remains quiet, except for the silent tears of Tanzy. Zipp searches for answers to inner questions of self-love, self-hatred, and yearning to believe each deserves to be loved the right way minus sex but intimacy.

EXT. 3AM CEDAR GROVE CEMENTARY AUGUSTA'S BLACK CEMENTARY

Zipp is dressed in all black with a back derby and is carrying a shovel and a curved icepick. Zipp is walking through the graveyard, each time he gets light from the moon he pauses and looks at the newspaper and inspects each head stone. Zipp finds the headstone he wants, then proceeds to sketch on a writing pad the exact duplicate of the headstone, flowers etc., that center's around the gravesite. He also measures the amount of dirt on the spot. Zipp shovels the dirt to the left side of the grave keeping all the dirt to one side. After twenty minutes, he hits the coffin. Using the shovel, Zipp is able to puncture a hole in the top of the front of the coffin. Once the hold has been completely opened without regard for the corpse, Zipp takes his curved icepick and jams the pointed end into the chin of the corpse just above the throat. Zipp is able to lift the corpse from the coffin grabbing it with both hands, places the corpse into a burlap bag, and places the corpse on to a covered wagon. Each night before 7am, Zipp is able to secure five cadavers.

With precision, Zipp is able to replace all the items including the dirt just the way the grave was left without error minus the corpse and a flower from the gravesite. Zipp's collection of weekly cadavers serves the lab to prepare each daily dissection.

THERE IS A SERIES OF SHOTS WITH ZIPP ROBBING GRAVES AND PLACING EACH BACK THE WAY THEY WERE.

From each grave after the fresh bodies have been exhumed, and the body removed from the coffin, then the coffins are placed back into the ground and the dirt and flowers replaced, Zipp always snips off a flower from each grave site for himself as his reminder that the bodies have been removed and which graves were robbed.

INT. SUNDAY MORNING SERVICE ZIPP IS SITTING IN THE PEWS.

Zipp is dress impeccably similar to a 19th century physician. Prior to the church service beginning (music is played) men and women of the congregation are making a sincere effort to greet Zipp. Women are especially attempting to flirt with him because of his clothing and status in the church. While the church music is playing, a collection basket is circulating the room. People are subtly watching how much people place in the basket. The basket reaches Zipp, who automatically reaches into his inside suit jacket pocket and extracts his billfold. Zipp selectively pulls out multiple bills and toss them inside the basket, then passes it to his neighbor. Immediate after that Zipp adjust his clandestine flower on his lapel. In the audience, Olive watches Zipp and enjoys the service.

The pastor walks to the podium and address the congregation.

> PASTOR
> Before we begin our festivities today and celebrate the Lord's Day, we
> have to address the events in our current circumstances.

There is a slight roar of agreement from the congregation underneath the soft instrumental gospel music.

> PASTOR (CONT'D)
>
> It has come to our attention that for some strange reason and God
> knows the reason because we don't know. Somebody has been
> stealing our dead!

There is a horrific scream amongst the congregants. Everyone is a great deal more attentive to the Pastor as he continues.

PASTOR (CONT'D)

I'm not certain when it started to happen, but members of our
community ventured out to clean the gravestones for their dearly
departed families and they noticed some of the headstones were ajar.
Now our member didn't pay too much attention to it, but she looked
around and notice the dirt didn't look like old dirt. It looked like it had
been stirred up. Now this time and age, we have some members in the
congregation that perhaps can talk to the white folks about our
cemetery and what colored people don't do. Can I get an amen brother
deacon Zipp?

Zipp looks up from his meditation on the Pastor's word and nods that he'd attempt through his influence, to find out who's been stealing slave bodies. The congregation sees the exchange and lightly applauses, although some don't. One raises his hand. The pastor acknowledges him and waves the congregation to cease the noise, indicating the gentleman has the floor.

CONGREGANT

Pastor! Thank you for acknowledging me. I too had my great
granddaddy stolen from Cedar Grove, but I just want to let somebody
know I'm building grave fences with a lock and key. It's buried in the
ground and only I got the key, and if whoever tries to grave-rob, they're
going to have a hard time and making loud noises trying to get in.

PASTOR

That's a great idea from a member of our congregation.

The congregants applaud at the successful idea presented. Zipp also applauds at the idea but sinisterly looks back at the congregation member with distain.

INT. ZIPP'S SHACK DAY.

Zipp takes off his bowtie and Tanzy is bringing his lunch to a table. The distinction between her clothing and his is extreme. After he takes off his jacket, he hands her the graveyard picked flower. Tanzy takes the flower and pins it to the inside of a curtain near the window, which displays many other pinned flowers old and new but a spectacular view.

TANZY

Zipp, can I go to church?

Zipp snaps a look at her from his elsewhere thought. He calms himself as she continually sets the table. Olive remains in the distance watching.

ZIPP

You do go to the church down town with all the other colored people, I'm not certain what you're referring to.

Tanzy and Zipp exchange glances, and she continues.

TANZY

I'm not sure what those fancy doctor words you are saying, but you know what I mean.

Zipp sits down at the table and Tanzy brings over the meal of cabbage, mushrooms, rice and onion soup. Zipp smiles and slices the brown bread.

ZIPP

It looks great!

Tanzy sits down to join him on opposite sides of the table and they clasp hands and bow their heads in prayer. Olive takes the moment and closes her eyes in prayer also.

TANZY

I want to look good like you when I go to church.

Zipp looks at Tanzy sarcastically.

ZIPP

What sense would that make, if you the only one dressed like a sophisticated lady at your church, people would start to wonder, where in the world did this woman from nowhere come up with some money from somewhere.

TANZY

Then take me to your church. They have a lot of high-class colored people that dress up like you, even though everybody knows you the best!

Zipp lightly smiles at the thought.

ZIPP

We are not married! I just can't show up with a sophisticated lady and everybody will start asking questions of you and me.

There is a moment of silence and both look at each other.

ZIPP (CONT'D)

Before you go making no decision about anything, I'm not marrying know
body because they dress nice and I don't expect you to either. It's bad
enough you staying here on your way to Philadelphia, and the good book
say we are not suppose to show an appearance of evil and then I show up
with you at the church, then my reputation will cause a stir. I'm a deacon
you know!

Tanzy looks sadden, but still presses on!

TANZY

Are you ready for me to be on my way? Who going to make you that red
cabbage, sautéed mushrooms and African cornbread?

Zipp and Tanzy share a laugh and they both dive in to their meal. After a moment of eating, they continue.

TANZY (CONT'D)

Can you at least get me some more clothes? Aren't you tired of seeing
me in the same stuff from my barrel ride? I know I'm tired of seeing it.
What would you like to see me in?

Zipp pauses immediate between bites and considers it.

ZIPP

I can get you something.

Tanzy quickly jumps on the opening, shoveling more cabbage and mushrooms on Zipp's plate. Zipp enjoys the
additional helpings.

TANZY

Did you mean something or some things?

Zipp sighs and gulps at the clarification.

ZIPP

Something!

A smiles crosses Tanzy's face as she begins to clear the table. She has a hop in her step, like a new prospective
bride has just been given an engagement ring.

Zipp rises from the table and puts on his smoking jacket which Tanzy just handed to him he heads to his reading
chair and stops at the library and selects a book and just about to sit.

TANZY

Oh, can you please make sure one of those things that you going to buy be is a mirror, I don't know how you get dressed without one. A woman needs a mirror.

Upon the word mirror Olive is at attention, waiting for
Zipp's response. Zipp is dejected

ZIPP

I avoid mirrors

TANZY

Why? Is it the way you look, your height?

Zipp sinks into the chair staring nowhere.

ZIPP

I had to fight all my life and until I couldn't fight! I had to fight other slaves making fun of me, I had to fight and run away because the circus was after me. I had to stay in the fields and be a quiet darkie. I couldn't fight the white man because he'd kill me. I hated myself and looking at myself remind me of myself, when I don't see myself, I can be who I am in my mind, my books, my lab, my job. Even though I know I'm the shortest and the not so best looking, but the doctors look up to me. I got respect for the first time and I going to keep it. Keep the mirror away from me, it will be yours, because from what I read about women, they like to dress and look at themselves and you something to look at.

Olive is still attentive. Tanzy smiles and walks over and hugs Zipp, he is little awkward in the embrace.

INT. Medical College of Georgia Ballroom evening.

Zipp is dressed in a black tuxedo similar to all of the physicians in attendance. He is the only black person dressed in that manner. There are other blacks present, however, they are dressed as servants and serving the physicians. Light classical instrumental is playing from a live band. Male students and physicians are engaged in different conversations.

Tanzy is also present, although, she is present as in a slave's capacity. Tanzy is walking around the various rooms with a tray of finger foods and wine. She circles the room smiling and serving. She sees Zipp in a corner surrounded by physicians who are all enthralled by his knowledge of cadavers, anatomy, physiology and organ procurement. Tanzy's height also allows her to see over people, including some physicians, therefore, so not to intimidate any male she walks with a bent over tilt and pretends she is docile and uninformed. Tanzy and Zipp eyes meet and he diverts his eyes as she approaches the semi-circle of conversation. She serves the small group.

TANZY

Would any of you doctors like a light refreshment before dinner is served?

The physicians look up at her and Tanzy quickly lowers herself and head. They begin taking food and wine from her tray. Tanzy positions the tray toward each physician, then toward Zipp, smiling widely. As oppose to the white doctors. Zipp immediately rebuffs the smile and her advances. He abruptly begins another conversation and the physicians engage again as if nothing has changed, closing the semicircle and edging Tanzy out. Tanzy obviously rejected moves away and stands at the back of the wall along with the other hired slave help. They acknowledge her and her tears.

FEMALE HIRED SLAVE

This your first time serving at MCG graduation?

Tanzy nods her head yes, as rejected tears stream down her face.

FEMALE HIRED SLAVE (CONT'D)

You will get use to the boss man talking to you and having his way with you!

TANZY

I'm use to that! You know a slave woman don't have no rights.

The female hired slave nods agreeing with Tanzy as they both survey the room to make certain everyone is content as other servants distribute the light snacks.

TANZY (CONT'D)

What I don't understand is . . .

The female hired slave interrupt her.

FEMALE HIRED SLAVE

Oh! You mean that Uncle Tom, he thinks he's one of them! I know him.
He's at my sister's church. He gives and make a lot money working for
MCG. My sister and me don't care for him too much.

Tanzy wipes away her tears and her attention is directed towards the woman.

TANZY

What's wrong with him? What happen?

The woman looks left and right then inches closer to Tanzy and whispers.

FEMALE HIRED SLAVE

My sister fell asleep early one night and she woke up in the middle of the night. She realized she left her washed clothes on the line. She ventured outside to get them off the line, because she did not want the morning dew to wet them again.

EXT. CEDAR GROVE CEMEMTARY NIGHT FLASH BACK

Zipp is standing at the front of the grave. The casket is positioned with the lower half in the grave itself. The upper half is protruding out. Zipp uses the shovel to punch a hole and create an opening in the casket. Zipp reaches in and touches the corpse with his hands and has difficulty pulling it out. He then pulls out his ice pick and yanks it out. He puts the body on his shoulder and then stuffs it in a bag. He looks back at the casket and reaches inside again and this time he pulls out the body of a dead baby. Zipp holds the baby in his arms reaches into his pocket and pulls out a flask. Zipp then places the flowers and the dirt back to the way it was and then he stops at another grave and continues.

INT. MEDICAL COLLEGE OF GEORGIA BALL ROOM MOMENTS LATER

FEMALE HIRED SLAVE

My sister said she's sure it was him, because he's the only one she knows that wears a black derby at night. Plus she said when he drank from his flask, he held his head up and the moon light hit his face. She said she made a noise and he looked in her direction. She said she froze in the dark, because he looked in her direction, but darkness hid her. Don't ever shake his hand!

Tanzy looks at her curiosity at such an odd statement.

TANZY

What's wrong with his hands?

The female hired slaves shudder at the thought, spinning around although not drawing attention to herself. She almost faints, but Tanzy stabilizes her.

FEMALE HIRED SLAVE

It takes you under. His hands are cold. He looks through you, not at

you, like he waiting on you to be in the ground so that he can snatch
your body in the moonlight for MCG.

There is a sound of someone tapping on a wine glass, attempting to get everyone's attention. The room settles down and everyone ceases their conversation. Physician One has the floor and address the graduates and physicians.

ONE PHYSICIAN

As senior physician here at MCG, I'd like to propose a toast to the
graduating newly minted doctors from the Medical College of Georgia for
the year of 1860. Although our country is divided, the South will prevail
and our way of life will be preserved. Keep practicing your craft!

The crowd lets a loud cheer and lift their glasses in a toast and agreement. A photographer appears and stands at a distance pointing out where each physician should stand in the picture. The photographer proposes that they all adjust to a ballroom set of stairs which allows them to be in a better tier position. Once they all are assembled, Zipp is standing alone off to the right, completely out of the picture. He has a piece of paper he is reading. Just as the photographer is preparing to take the shot, several newly minted physicians murmur amongst themselves. It grabs the attention of Physician One.

ONE PHYSICIAN (CONT'D)

Zipp!

Zipp looks up from his reading material, as all the physicians motion for Zipp to join them in the picture. Zipp goes to the very top of the step adjacent to other physicians. The photographer counts down from five to one and as the picture is about to flash Zipp holds up his paper in the midst of the shot.

INT. ZIPP'S SHACK EVENING

Zipp is in his lounge chair reading. Tanzy is pulling the iron in and out of the fire place. She is pressing Zipp's custom shirts. Zipp glances over to her and she doesn't catch his attention. When she does look over, he doesn't catch her attention. There is an eerie silence among the two. Tanzy breaks the ice.

TANZY

It was nice they put you in the picture, wasn't it?

Zipp glances over, responds by murmuring yes, then goes back to his reading. Tanzy puts the iron back in the fire and approaches Zipp. She standing over him and he looks up at her. They both realize her height in this instance and is almost meant to intimidate. She sits down across from him.

TANZY (CONT'D)

Did they give you a diploma like the other doctors? I saw you hold it up
when the picture was taken? Now that you taught me how to read, I

want to read it. I never seen a diploma up close, only at the white folk
house hanging on the wall.

Zipp, contemplatively reaches into his inside pocket and hands Tanzy the sheets of paper. Tanzy excitedly receives the paper and begins slowly and methodically reads. Her smile changes to a solemn expression then looks toward Zipp. She stands and walks backward toward the fire place with the paper work in her hand still deciphering the words.

TANZY (CONT'D)

This don't sound like graduation paperwork. It has your name but . . .

Zipp stands and walks toward Tanzy. She looks confused. She turns her back and grabs the extremely hot iron and sears her hand. Dropping the iron immediately while holding on to the paper. Zipp runs to the eating area, grabs some lard, places it in her hand and rubs it in her hand. Zipp takes the paper and places it on the iron board and leads her over to the chairs. They both sit. In between her pains from the burns, Tanzy responds.

TANZY (CONT'D)
Thank you for helping me. What are those papers?

Zipp sighs and takes a deep breath!

ZIPP

Those papers are my freedom papers. I'm no longer a slave, I'm free. I am a man to go to and from where ever I can.

TANZY
You haven't been a slave as long as I've been here! You got white folk
clothes. You got a job that they pay you to do. Even black folks are sort of
afraid of you. Everybody shows you respect in Augusta, Georgia. Tell me
what you do?

Olive is still present, watching and waiting. Zipp is a little perturbed by the question. He walks away, goes to his closet, pulls out a large box and drops it at the feet of Tanzy.

She looks up at him then down at the box with one hand in pain and the other free. She wipes the lard off her clothing and gingerly she opens the box and carefully takes out beautiful colored lace dress and clothing of a lady from that era. She stands and holds it around her body.

Olive stands and moves closer. Tanzy sits down and neatly places the items from the box across another chair and looks at the combs, brushes and a small hand held mirror. She looks at herself as she brushes her hair.

TANZY (CONT'D)
I don't have long hair. My hair has always been naturally short.

Zipp lightly smiling.

ZIPP

Hair don't make you and you are not your hair.

Tanzy smiles brightly, but then becomes contemplative.

TANZY

Thank you. People are talking about you! They saying you do things other than doctor stuff at night to dead slaves.

Zipp a little angry that his secret is leaking out, shouts not at Tanzy but at the circumstances.

ZIPP

Would you rather I go back to the being a field slave, house slave, or a dead slave? I'm working. I'm getting money! The college paying me to be a porter. That's all you know and I know! There are parts of every job people don't like! What I did and what I do caused me to be a freeman. Sometimes when you plant wheat in the ground, the weeds come up with them. God knows I rather be the wheat than the weeds.

Olive circles the room trying to get a glace of the mirror Tanzy still has in her hand. She cannot see it. Tanzy places the mirror face down on the chair with the new clothing it.

Tanzy smiles at Zipp, who walks over, grabs his freedom papers and inserts it into his inside pocket. He turns and looks at Tanzy who is amazed at the items in the box.

Footsteps are heard approaching the shack. Zipp and Tanzy freeze. Then Zipp motions for her to get behind a curtain and remain still. There is a loud knock at the door. Zipp scans the room and sees the women's clothing on the chair and rushes over and places them on the floor in the box obviously wrinkling them. Tanzy watches from the curtain and covers her mouth in despair at the thought of her new clothes being wrinkled. Zipp gets to the door and unlocks it and the Third Physician enters the room surveying the room.

THIRD PHYSICIAN

Greetings Zipp!

ZIPP

Good greeting sir. How can I help you?

Zipp is taken aback by the abruptness of Third Physician entering his shack but he keeps his control.

THIRD PHYSICIAN

Yes, I've never been in a slave cave, excuse me a former slave's dwelling.
I see we have don't quite well for you since you been our porter.

ZIPP

Yes sir and I thank you. Is there something I can get for you sir? I can get my
keys and we can meet in the lab right now.

Zipp attempts to leave, hoping the doctor will follow him but he doesn't. He continues to survey the room looking at the books on Zipp's bookshelf.

THIRD PHYSICIAN

No Zipp, what I have to say, we can say right here.

The doctors stand directly in front of Zipp trying to intimidate because of the height difference.

THIRD PHYSICIAN (CONT'D)

The school has done quite well, however, this year and the years coming
and other colleges are starting to recruit many of our students from
Georgia to different Medical Schools across this country.

THIRD PHYSICIAN (CONT'D)

With the thoughts running through the country concerning the North and
South fighting a war, we want to keep our good-ole- boys coming to MCG
medical schools not going elsewhere. So, you know our type of planting
and harvest season is coming and we recruiting new students about the
same time to arrive this winter when planting season is over and our
barreled harvest will come in we'll do well right?

Zipp shakes his head at the long dialogue, but listen intently. Third Physician winks his eye at Zipp and smiles deceptively.

ZIPP

Yes, sir how can I help.

THIRD PHYSICIAN

Good! We have some barrels coming in to the dock. Get some local
specimens. Some of the state colleges are charging us different rates.

We need you to help with the exchange, get more barrels and parts in
here in the name of medical advancement and have them harvested by
next student admission before winter.

By this time the Third Physician is at the door and he exits. Zipp locks the door and goes over to Tanzy's clothing
and begins reassembling them on the chair. Tanzy comes over and she takes over and Zipp flops in his chair
looking at her.

ZIPP

We going to have to get hitched! Tanzy snaps a wide grin at Zipp, then it turns into a frown.

TANZY

A slave can't marry a free man! Can she? What about your job? You have
to get more barrels from here and the docks!

ZIPP

A big wedding will help. We'll invite everybody. I'll pay for everything.
We'll have food and whisky. A big party. The get together will take their
minds off me. I'll get your freedom papers! Are you still going to
Philadelphia?

Unsuspecting of the question, Tanzy is stunned by the question and her children. She begins to tear up but then
gains her composure. She stares at Zipp while sitting down.

TANZY

A woman never forgets the child she had and never stops wondering about
her child's birthday, or if the child thinks about her. Who raising the child
and if she or he is a slave, free, dead or alive, only gone?

Zipp comes closer and places his hand on her shoulder, this time he is standing above her, assuring her.

ZIPP

The country is about to fight a war. There is no way to know how long
the war is going to last. A woman traveling alone from Georgia to
Philadelphia is dangerous.

TANZY

Come with me!

Zipp paces the room, and begins to switch clothing. He goes to the other side of the room and undresses. Tanzy
respects his privacy. Zipp speaks from the other side of the curtain.

ZIPP

My job is here. I can't get no other job like this for a former slave. I'd
have to travel some slave states just to get to a free state. It's too risky
and are you certain your children are in Philadelphia?

Tanzy's head drops and she remains silent.

Zipp emerges from beyond the curtain. He is dressed in customary clandestine uniform and heads for the door.
He looks at Tanzy whose head remains dejected. You know where I'm going. I'll be back in a while after stopping
at the lab. I know your earth and your heaven is mixed up right now. Is there anything I can bring you back when
I return?

Tanzy remains silent as Zipp opens and exits the door. Just as the door closes shut and Zipp is a few feet away.
Zipp's shack door opens slowly and he turns around surprised at the door opening. Tanzy pokes her head out in
to the moonlight and softly whispers.

TANZY

A tall mirror so I can see all of myself.

Zipp nods his head and pulls his derby over his eyes and walks into the moonlight darkness. Olive excitedly
jumps and with anticipation at hearing about the mirror.

EXT. 3AM BRUSH PARTIALLY DEVELOPED LAND NEAR CEDAR GROVE CEMENTARY

Zipp is walking confidently in the moon lit darkness. In a distance he is able to see lit lanterns coming toward a
clearing in multiple directions. He pauses for a moment and listens to the sound of the footsteps crackling the
forest earth. Zipp takes a deep breath and continues onward. There is a clearing in a distance and in the middle
of the clearing there is a small fire burning and several white men gather around. The flames from everyone's
lantern provides the light to the event. Zipp approaches the group and he is immediately ignored and the men
begin the subtle dialogue between each other. All of the men have on varied colored sweaters with different
insignia from various universities across the country. After about ten of the men are assembled, one man
dressed in crimson addresses the group. CRIMSON stands on a soap box as the others and Zipp gather around.

CRIMSON

Let's begin the negotiations. What are opening bids for a dead adult male
darkie?

Several men shout out!

CROWD SHOUTING

5 dollars or 6 dollars!

Crimson drops his head then shakes it.

CRIMSON

Brothers we all know the males and females are worth more!

INDIGO

Each university needs plenty of specimens. How else are we going to compete with the foreign medical schools? Our sons will go abroad and practice there.

Zipp asserts himself in the middle of the conversation. When he speaks, everyone gazes at him, whispering amongst themselves about which school does he represent.

ZIPP

Shouldn't we consider what the cadaver's body has endured alive and the time table before decomposition before we label a sales price?

There is a slow murmur of agreement amongst the leaders, and all look at Crimson for a response. Crimson throws a glance at Zipp then responds.

CRIMSON

Yes, our guest is from . . .

Looking at Zipp to introduce which school he represents the other negotiators.

ZIPP

MCG

There is a murmur amongst the crowd at the thought of a black man representing one of the southern states in negotiations for slave cadavers.

Crimson notices the atmosphere is changing while everyone is focusing on Zipp's role. He taps a gavel on a tree stump near him to bring the attention back to him and negotiations.

CRIMSON

Yes, MCG is correct, therefore, what are the proposals?

Another leader steps to the front of the conversation.

AZURE

Gentlemen, gentlemen, we each obviously represent our medical investors quite well, and we want to return to our respective establishments as soon as possible.

AZURE (CONT'D)

I suggest we prepare a standard price for adults, mothers with children and children alone without the ongoing negotiations. Time is of the essence.

EMERALD

Nice speech, my colleague, but I did not hear you mention any numbers. Can we be more specific in terms of cost than policies?

Crimson looks around the clearing at each patron and hammers again his gavel on the tree stump. Everyone ceases their conversation and pays attention to Crimson.

CRIMSON

Is there anyone here representing the slave owner's commission?

There is a shout from back in the bushes and everyone turns in the direction of the dark bushes as several footsteps approach. Out of the darkness appears two men in full Klansmen regalia. The male college negotiators open the circle and the two Klansmen walk to the center of the group looking at Crimson. Zipp, slowly and methodically backs into the bushes, hidden and remaining silent. One of the Klansmen addresses the audience.

KLANSMAN

We're sorry for being a little late, as you can see, we been a busy chasing niggers.

He wipes off his Klan robe from the dirt and swings a noose like a lasso.

I know some of you are Yankees and Jews. Don't worry, we just after niggers tonight, but if you stay too long in Georgia, after tonight then we'll get you.

The other Klansman with his rifle on his shoulder nudges the other, towards Zipp direction but they are not certain because of the darkness. Zipp backs up a little more and more so not to be seen. The first Klansmen believes his cohort wants him to continue on with negotiations.

Look, we got the supply and you want the demand. We are going to set the prices!

KLANSMAN (CONT'D)

We heard you, selling dead slaves' body-parts across America, and with a war pending that the south will win! We keeping slavery. We still going to make money off every dead slave property. Where else you going to go to, the abolitionists?

Both Klansmen chuckle at the sarcastic joke. Crimson clears his throat and the Klansmen turns their attention to Crimson looking up at him from the forest floor at the soap box. Zipp steps backward deeper into the forest. He looks up at the moon light and is confused with his directions, not wanting to go back the way he entered. He remains within earshot.

> CRIMSON
>
> Sir, with all due respect to the south can you provide a price to the slave
> crop and allow us to be able to meet our demand for the medical school
> recruitment admissions?

The two Klansmen look at each other for clarification and ignore Crimson. Point their rifle at him and he stiffens and remains silent.

> KLANSMAN
>
> I don't know what you said Yankee boy and stop hitting that stump with
> that hammer and shut up and listen.

The other Klansmen hands the main Klansmen a piece of paper. The second Klansmen is still surveying the area for intruders. He begins to circle the group with his rifle off his shoulder cocked and ready. The group's attention is diverting between listening to the first Klansmen's price list and the other pacing the semi-circle. He has difficulty reading the list but the point is understood

> KLANSMAN
>
> Inky kids, ages 4-10, eight dollars each. Mammies and Pickaninnies
> together- we charging 15 dollars for both. If they a wench or a buck
> alone we charging a straight 12 dollars.

There is a small murmur of disappointment amongst the crowd but no one dares to disagree.

The Klansman guarding the area scans the area and looks toward where Zipp was standing, sees the movement and walks rapidly towards where Zipp was standing. The other Klansmen sees his cohort about to run and follows him. He lets out a yell then shoots his gun in the air. Running in the forest.

> This meeting is about over!

The sound of the shotgun blast causes everyone to scatter, in various directions. The Klansmen race toward Zipp. Still not sure who they are chasing but closing rapidly. Two gentlemen from the different school meet up in the bushes still walking briskly toward their carriages. Crimson and Azure meet at their wagons.

> AZURE
>
> What do we do now?

Sadden, shook, but relieved that he is in his carriage about to take off into the darkness.

> CRIMSON
>
> We have to pay. They set the prices. They have the product. We need the students. The south has too many advantages right now. The war is certain now.

> AZURE
>
> Do you think the president will grant freedom to the slaves?

Crimson readies his reins in hands for the gallop of the horses as does Azure.

> CRIMSON
>
> Slaves I don't know. I think he'll do what is economically profitable to unite the states.

Each snap their horse to attention and dash into the darkness.

EXT. ZIPP IN THE FORREST RUNNING

The Klansmen running after Zipp, who are laughing and shooting their guns into the sky. Zipp believes they are shooting at him and is constantly ducking and moving from side to side trying to avoid being shot. He is jumping up and over different logs and branches and trees. As Zipp runs through the forest, he sees another clearing and deeper bushes beyond the clearing.

Zipp hears the Klansmen footsteps behind him and he darts toward the edge of the other bushes and a loud noise causes Zipp to look behind him but he sees nothing. Zipp turns forward and views in the middle of the field a burning cross and another 40 Klansmen dressed in regalia looking in his direction. Zipp freezes as the two Klansmen though out of breath catch up with him and grab both his arms and walk him toward the enormous burning cross. The other Klansmen surround him. One Klansmen knocks his derby to the ground and the shouts out racial epithets in the darkness. In the darkness, another Klansmen rides up on a horse with a lynch rope and lassos the robe around Zipp's neck and quickly walks him toward a large tree. The light from the burning cross brightens the event that is about to happen. All of the Klansmen walk over to the tree that the rope has been tossed around. Zipp's hands have been tied and his mouth gagged. As the group of Klansmen walk over toward the tree, they trample over Zipp's derby. One Klansman picks it up but continues on. A couple of Klansmen help get Zipp atop the horse and make certain the rope is tightened around his neck. One stands adjacent to the horse rump awaiting the signal to strike the horse. The Klansmen with the derby in his hand steps forward, looking sternly at Zipp.

> THIRD KLANSMEN
>
> Where did you get this derby?

Zipp tries to speak, through the stuffed handkerchief in his mouth, frighten and stuttering. The Klansmen motions for another to remove the handkerchief and he does so. Coughing, gaging and out of breath Zipp speaks.

                        ZIPP

Yes, sir. That's mine sir!

                    THIRD KLANSMEN

You sure boy? If you lying and stole this derby from that boy-porter
from MCG, we going to hog tie you and cut you like a bull that can't
make no more calves.

Zipp shakes his head vehement as tears roll from his eyes.

                        ZIPP

That's mine sir! That's mine!

A shout from the crowd frightens Zipp even more!

                    CROW SHOUTING

He lying, just hang him, just hang him. We could sell him to those Yankees.

                        ZIPP

No sir that's my derby. It fits my head. Let me try it on, sir. Let me try it on
for size! It will fit my head.

The Klansmen tosses to the other klansmen and he catches it. Zipp leans down from the horse. The horse stirs
and almost gallops, tightening the rope. Zipp, swallows hard and breathes heavy trying to get some air in. The
Klansmen places the hat on his head and it fits with precision.

                    THIRD KLANSMEN

I'm not convinced this smart dressing nigger with a derby ain't who he
says he is!

The crowd murmurs as the horse paces in front of the crowd and the Third Klansman contemplates. He stops
and pauses, then begins pacing with the horse, then he responds.

                 THIRD KLANSMEN (CONT'D)

Tell me something medical, then I know you are who you say you are!

Zipp swallows hard and is shaking on the horse who looks up at him and can detect his fear. Zipp takes a deep
breath.

THIRD KLANSMEN (CONT'D)

Come on boy, you got something to say or not?

ZIPP

Yes sir! Yes sir! The human body is made up of about 6 different sections and within each section are different organizational structures. The skeletal, muscular, cardiovascular respiratory, digestive and urinary systems. Each of these fight off disease and respond to different environmental challenges.

The Klansmen pauses then looks at Zipp, holds up his hands and Zipp stops. He motions for the other Klansmen to take Zipp down from the horse. All of the group of Klansmen are bewildered by Zipp's knowledge. The rope is removed from his neck which now has swollen scar and his hands are untied. The derby remains on his head.

The Klansmen a little dejected all turn around and head back toward the burning cross, while drinking, laughing and applauding each other. The Third Klansmen remains looking at Zipp.

THIRD KLANSMEN

You still had a good night nigger. You lived and you earned some fresh money for you and MCG.

The Klansmen turns and walks towards the others and away from burning cross. Zipp, who immediately drops to his knees, puts his hands in prayer mode. The shadow light from the moon and burning cross reflects to Zipp's right as a wind blows a shifting swinging shadow and sound of tree branches. Zipp turns around and looks to the far left in the shadow of the moon. There are four black people swinging from a tree. A mother, daughter, father and a son hanging in the night wind. Zipp takes off his derby and weeps. Then reaches into his pocket and pulls out a pocket knife and body bags.

INT. ZIPP'S SHACK EARLY MORNING LATER THAT MORNING

Zipp enters his residence. He is exhausted. He looks toward the blanket separating his section from Tanzy section. He hears her singing and attempts to slip into his cot quietly. She snatches the side of her curtain and spots him. He still covers himself completely.

TANZY

Thank you so much.

Tanzy exits her side of the room and has a dress draped around her. She walks over and sits on the edge of the cot close to Zipp. Zipp's head is covered. Tanzy lightly pulls on the covers. There is a small resistance. She pulls a little harder and Zipp relents. They look at each other. Tanzy stands and models for Zipp. He is amazed and a slight smile comes across his face. Tanzy kneels to his bedside face to face. They lightly kiss each other upon the lips. Then Zipp pulls away as the kisses become a little more passionate. Tanzy backs away also wondering.

> TANZY (CONT'D)
>
> What is wrong?

Zipp looks at her then shakes his head, and becomes more dejected.

> TANZY (CONT'D)
>
> We are engaged. We'll be getting hitched real soon. It's ok!

Zipp again shakes his head no, then looks at her and grabs her hand tightly.

> ZIPP
>
> You don't have to do this!

Tanzy interrupts.

> TANZY
>
> I want to. You've been taking care of me just like a husband should. I
> don't lack for anything. You haven't asked for nothing. Why? Those slave
> owners took me, took my children and took me again. I was their bed
> warmer. Now I want to be yours!

Zipp sits up on the cot. Tanzy is on her knees looking at him face to face. Zipp takes a deep breath, pauses.

> ZIPP
>
> I don't own you. Yes, I do love you and I believe you love me. For the first
> time in my life, I love us enough not to spoil our wedding night. I been
> without a woman, since some unknown woman had me. Waiting a little
> while longer is not going to make a difference. You been taken so many
> times, now it's time you receive me in the right way.

Tanzy smiles and they kiss each other and embrace, as Tanzy hugs Zipp, she notices the fresh scar on his neck. She jumps up away from him.

> TANZY
>
> What happened to your neck?

She tenderly touches all around his neck and Zipp winces in pain at her touch. He examines his neck with his hands and creates more pain. Tanzy grabs Zipp by the hand and pulls him toward her side of the room.

INT. TANZY SIDE OF THE ROOM MOMENTS LATER

Tanzy's side is decorated in a feminine manner, yet leaning against the wall backwards is a large full-length mirror. In her concern to show Zipp and his weariness of the day, both have forgotten his early decree.

                    TANZY

    Look in the mirror!

When the words are mentioned, Olive comes out of a corner and darts toward the other side of the room. She stands attentive waiting for the mirror to be revealed. Tanzy unveils the mirror, and turns it forward and holds it so Zipp can see the severe rope burns from the attempted lynching. He attempts to touch it again and light bleeding commences. Tanzy tilts the mirror against a wall and leaves. Zipp continues to examine his neck. Tanzy returns with a damp cloth and daps at the wicked scar bleeding and swelling. The swelling subsides. Tanzy then grabs one of her scarfs and places around Zipp's neck like an ascot. Then gets Zipp's smoking jacket and helps him into the jacket.

Tanzy appears adjacent to Zipp in the mirror. They look at each other through the mirror. Both of their eyes are on each other. Tanzy looks at her self-standing above Zipp and attempts to stoop down to balance the picture. Zipp urges her to stand her normal size and she does so.

                    ZIPP

    You really make me look good in a mirror!

Olive tries to get closer, but both characters are indirectly blocking her from entering the mirror. She also is exhausted and dragging around the room, trying to locate a way to return back to her life. Zipp, leans the mirror back against the wall and returns to his side of the room, Tanzy goes to the kitchen area and begins to prepare a morning meal for Zipp. Olive approaches the full-length mirror and attempts to step inside. Suddenly Tanzy returns and quickly and tenderly, snatches the mirror and flips it backwards and rewraps a blanket around it for safe keeping. Olive is devastated and drops to the floor on her knees. She begins praying seeking an answer.

Throughout the rest of the story, Zipp continues to wear a colorful ascot or shirt and tie hiding the swollen noose scar.

INT. MCG-LAB OFFICE. DAY

Physician One, Crimson, Azure, and Zipp are in a meeting. The door is closed. Outside the operation of a cadaver lab classes are operating as usual. All are sitting except Zipp, who waits for Physician One to motion for him to sit. He does so after light talk amongst the two northern gentlemen and Physician One. Zipp remains silent. Each has a leather-bound satchel.

Crimson reaches into his satchel and removes a small gavel and lightly hammers on the table get their attention and everyone simmers down. Zipp has remained quiet.

CRIMSON

Gentlemen and Zipp, thank you for coming to this meeting. I do appreciate
the accommodations in Georgia and we hope not to hold you to longer, or
ourselves, because of this blistering Georgia heat.

Crimson taps Zipp's shoulder.

Zipp, can you go get us a cold glass of . . .

Zipp attempts to rise from the table to do as told, but the thought hits him and he sits down again. Crimson looks at his colleagues bewildered.

ZIPP

I'm a free man, although Georgia is not free. I have papers to prove it! I
can tell you where the water pump is, if you want to know!

Physician one, smiles at Zipp, as the other two are speechless. Crimson shakes his head and changes subjects.

CRIMSON

Ok, the reason why we called this meeting centers around the way the country
is moving and the sincere possibility of a war between the states.

ONE PHYSICIAN

That's quite evident that the North is quite jealous of the economic gains of
the south.

AZURE

That's one of the reasons why we are here. All of the colleges up north
are performing internal audits. Laws are changing in the country and as
laws change our financial climate has to adapt.

CRIMSON

All of the schools could not schedule to be here today, but their financial
records are present.

Crimson and Azure place their bags on the desk simultaneously and begin opening them and pull several university and college insignia ledgers.

ONE PHYSICIAN

I understand, we also have to avoid any future liability to MCG and
continually evaluate risk factors.

For a moment there is a pause and the white men glance at Zipp, who acknowledges their pause, wanting his input. Zipp looks at each one eye to eye confidently.

ZIPP

In other words you want to know where, how, why, when, and what the
money is spent on?

They each look dumbfounded as Zipp pulls out his own beat-up satchel and pulls out his own black ledger.

Every dollar for all the slave cadavers and body parts shipped at MCG
are accountable.

Zipp slides his ledger to the center of the table scattering the other ledgers. Then the other gentlemen catch the ledgers. They slide the different ledgers to everyone around the room and everyone dives in the respective university financial records.

INT. SPRINGFIELD BAPTIST CHURCH AUGUSTA, GEORGIA DAY

Zipp is dressed in an impeccable tuxedo for the wedding ceremony. Tanzy has on a sensational wedding gown. They are standing in front of the minister, listening to him recite the instructions and responsibilities as husband and wife.

Behind the couple, there are scattered supporters on both sides of the church. Upper crust of blacks are sitting on Zipp's side of the church and onlookers are sitting on Tanzy side of the church. Olive is sitting in a pew, although no one can see her. The minster motions for the couple to face each other and they do, gazing into each other's eyes with love and excitement.

MINISTER

I need both the bride and groom to repeat after me when it's your turn.

He looks at Zipp initially. The minister speaks and Zipp repeats the words.

I Zipp Wind, take thee Tanzy Poston to be my wedded wife, to have and
to hold this day forward, for better or for worse, for richer or for
poorer, in sickness and in health, to love and to cherish, till death us do
part, according to God's Holy ordinance; and thereto I plight thee my
troth.

The minster motions that the couple take each hands and motions for Tanzy to follow his directions. Tanzy repeats after the minister.

I Tanzy Poston, take thee Zipp Wind, to be my wedded husband, to
have and to hold this day forward, for better or for worse, for richer or
for poorer, in sickness and in health, to love and to cherish, till death us
do part, according to God's Holy ordinance; and thereto I plight thee
my troth.

Zipp then gives the minister the rings and he is a little surprised at the ring that Zipp provides for Tanzy. She is also crestfallen by the gift for her marriage by Zipp. The minister regains his composure and continues. The minister holds the ring up above the bride and groom's head and prays.

> MINISTER (CONT'D)
>
> With this ring I thee wed: in the name of the Father and of the Son and of the Holy Spirit. Amen.

> The minister taps Zipp's and Tanzy's shoulder motioning for them to kneel on the towels placed on the floor below them. They each bow their heads reverently.

> MINISTER (CONT'D)
>
> O Almighty God, Creator of humankind, who only art the wellspring of life: bestow upon these thy servants, if it be thy will, the gift and heritage of children; and grant that they may see their children brought up in the faith and fear,

Tanzy shudders and tears flow from her veil.

> MINISTER (CONT'D)
>
> To the honor and glory of thy name; through Jesus Christ our Lord. Amen.

The minster finishes and Zipp stands and attempts to help Tanzy up but she is sobbing quite rapidly. She awkwardly stands to her feet as Zipp steadies her. He hands her his handkerchief and she blow her nose and wipes away her sporadic tears.

Zipp motions to the minister to speed up the process and he does and the couple exchanges rings. The minister then turns the couple to the congregation who stand sporadically. The minister speaks to the congregation.

> Ladies and gentlemen on April 12, 1861, for the first time I'd like to introduce to you Mr. and Mrs. Zipp and Tanzy Wind!

There is a light applause, as the couple exits the altar and escorts the small congregation and onlookers into a reception hall.

INT. SPRINGFEILD BAPTIST CHURCH RECEPTION HALL DAY

The couple enters the door and the room is filled with African American people, who are festive and drinking and dancing prior to the bride and groom entrance. The crowd glances at the couple entering and lets out an audible cheer, but is distracted by the beats and sounds and influence of alcohol, food and festivities. Tanzy is shocked and leans over to Zipp, who remains reserved, smiling and waves at various people.

> TANZY
>
> Why weren't these people at the wedding, at least for you?

Zipp grabs two drinks from a waiter passing by and Tanzy grabs two napkins simultaneously and hands one to Zipp as he hands her a drink.

> ZIPP
>
> They are not here for our wedding. They are here for the celebration.

> TANZY
>
> That bothers me!

Zipp interlocks the arms with the drinks so that she is drinking out of his glass and he out of hers. He whispers to her and kiss her lightly on the lips. She blushes and softens.

> ZIPP
>
> Just as long as they concern themselves with themselves and not what I do to
> take care of you, everything will work out fine.

The music plays on . . .

EXT. OUTSIDE OF SPRINGFIELD BAPTIST CHURCH 11:30 AM

The sound of several gunshots are heard which immediately silences the music and the wedding party participants remain still. The door to the church bursts open and a frantic black man with his satchel around his back looking afraid but anxious, continually watching behind him. He also barefoot but is excited! He shouts at the congregation!

> RUNAWAY SLAVE
>
> The Rebs just shot up and bombed
> Fort Sumter! Alabama, Mississippi, Florida, Georgia and Florida are all
> leaving the Union. I'm taking my family up North. Yawl better get going!
> There's no telling what them Rebs are going to do! I want to be a free
> man!

The statements by the runaway slave stills the congregants. He looks at them all stunned by his announcement. He reaches into his satchel and removes a small hand gun and points in everyone's direction.

If any of you slave niggers want to stay in the south, I'm fine with that,
just don't stop me!

RUNAWAY SLAVE (CONT'D)

Any of you want to be free come with me. If you try to stop me, I'll put
you in the ground where you stand!

The runaway darts away and we hear a horse gallop away. The congregants gather their composure and start leaving quickly. Some are grabbing food items and liquor for their journey. Some are sitting down and dumbfounded on what to do with their current situations. Tanzy looks around and people are scattered in all directions. She looks in all directions and can't find Zipp. She walks to the front door of the church.

EXT. SPRINGFIELD BAPTIST CHURCH AUGUSTA GEORGIA MOMENTS LATER

Standing at the top of the steps of church, Tanzy looks out of the town and black people are moving in all directions. Whites are screaming at blacks to adhere to their commands as slaves but some are not and some slaves remain obedient. A buggy pulls up in front of the church full of items and belongings. Zipp jumps off and runs up to Tanzy. She is relieved it's Zipp and comes downstairs. He helps her into the wagon and takes off down the road!

TANZY

Where are we going?

Tanzy shakes her head and takes a deep breath!

ZIPP

The war just started on our wedding day. I can't believe this. I have to be
more concerned about me now that I have you. I'm a free man and I got
the papers to prove it! You my wife and nobody's slave anymore! We
both will still be slaves if they catch us!

Zipp snaps the reins on the buggy and creates clouds of smoke down the road. Tanzy holds on to the buggy and fingers through the belonging Zipp has packed and she smiles that her mirror is still wrapped tightly. Adjacent to the mirror is a Morse code machine. Olive sits on the back of the buggy.

THE ARE A MONTAGE OF SHOTS DEPICTING SCENES OF THE CIVIL WAR
BATTLES. OLDER AND YONGER MEN FALLING ON THE FIELD OF BATTLE
FROM VARIOUS WOUNDS. THE GUN BATTLES ARE FEROCIOUS AND THE
MORTALLY WOODED ARE EITHER CARRIED AWAY OR REMAIN WHERE THEY WERE SLAIN. EACH YEAR OF THE FOUR-YEAR BATTLE IS DEPICTED.

EXT: CHARLOTTE, NORTH CAROLINA, DAY, OPEN FEILD 1865

Zipp is out harvesting the fields with other black farmers. They are walking behind their oxen and picking up the crops. Tanzy is a distance away hanging out laundry and scanning the country side. In a distance, she sees a horse galloping toward her rapidly. She backs off as the horse and the rider approaches. Tanzy glances behind her at Zipp and waves her hands and shouts in his direction. Zipp looks up and sees her frantic wave and darts toward her direction. He also sees the residual dust from the rider. Zipp snatches his shot gun and runs toward the rider, Tanzy and his house. The rider and Zipp reach Tanzy about the same time and Zipp's shot gun is drawn and pointed toward the young black male rider.

                    ZIPP

        Boy! Didn't your Father and Mother tell you never to ride up on a man or a
        woman across harvested land? You just destroy part of my share! What's
        wrong with you?

The young male rider is stunned at the shot-gun pointed at him and is frozen. He begins to hyperventilate and is unable to speak. He glances behind him bewildered at the crop filled land and dust he generated.

Tanzy pushes the gun's barrel as a threat downward and the young-man swallows hard. Zipp relents.

        Speak boy! Speak.

                    YOUNG MALE RIDER

        Yes sir!

He starts to stutter and is reassured more so when Tanzy looks at Zipp and he relents again.

                    YOUNG MALE RIDER (CONT'D)

        The war, the war!

The youth's horse paces back and forth, jumping to speed down the road!

                    ZIPP

        Yeah, we know about the war. Why did you trample over my field? If you
        were a grown man and did what you did, the owner of this land could
        have you shot!

Tanzy lightly touches Zipp's shoulder and he softens. As the young male rider speaks the sound of the horse disrupts the conversation. Zipp grabs the reins of the horse and calms the beast down petting it softly. The young male rider still shouts!

                    YOUNG MALE RIDER

        Sir the war, the war is over! The war is over! The south surrender.
        We are free!

Both Tanzy and Zipp are stunned by the news. Zipp lets the reins of the horse go and the horse dashes across the field kicking up more dirt and land that Zipp just harvested. Zipp and Tanzy embrace each other. Olive who has been standing there remains still watching the young male rider broadcast the news to different farmers across the field. Some walk across the field, some drop their equipment and what was harvested and dart towards their dwellings in jubilation.

Zipp and Tanzy walk into the house followed by Olive who moves through the walls and enters the house. They go into different directions and beginning packing individual things. Tanzy packs her lady things and Zipp is backing things in crates. The house is a great contrast from what they had. Olive comes close to Tanzy as she pulls out the mirror and Olive comes close to the mirror attempting to seize an opportunity to leap into it!

INT. ZIPP AND TANZY'S PLACE IN RURAL NORTH CAROLINA

> ZIPP
>
> There's no reason to unwrap the mirror now. We headed home.

Tanzy stops unwrapping and looks at Zipp. He doesn't notice she is not packing, consequently he continues to do so.

> TANZY
>
> The war is over! We are free!

Immediately after Tanzy speaks, the Morse code machine begins tapping out a message. Zipp deliberately drops what he was doing and jets to the table and begins transcribing the message.

> TANZY (CONT'D)
>
> That's the first time I heard that thing in all four years we've been here!
> I thought you brought it as a souvenir from the lab.

He continues to transcribe the message. Tanzy beings packing again, rewrapping the mirror, and Olive is flabbergasted.

> TANZY (CONT'D)
>
> Now that we free. We could go anywhere. We don't have to go south
> anymore! We could go north!

> ZIPP
>
> You mean north, like living in Philadelphia?

The couple glance at each other while packing. Tanzy shakes her head vehemently and begins packing.

> ZIPP (CONT'D)
>
> I don't know about that sweetheart. I just don't know.

Tanzy stops what she is doing and comes over and sits near Zipp. She motions for him to join her on the bed, but he refuses and continues to pack. She touches his hand slightly and he succumbs and they sit adjacent to one another. Tanzy holds both of Zipp's hand in hers.

> TANZY
>
> I have to go north! The war is over. A lot of people who were slaves are not slaves any more. We free!

> ZIPP
>
> You right sweetheart but we've been living here all of our lives. A lot of people you see going up North don't have a destination. The slaves use to being told what to do, where to go, and when to get up, although we worked, we had a roof over our heads.

Tanzy stands and slowly backs away from Zipp a bit baffled.

> TANZY
>
> Both our mommas and daddies were slaves. You sounded like a man that don't want to leave the plantation and his master!

Zipp stands and is highly insulted and returns to packing. Tanzy realizes she hurt him and comes over and touches his shoulder causing him to spin around. He adjusts his ascot but is reluctant to look at her eyes, but looks at his packing. Tanzy tilts his head up to get his attention and eye contact. Zipp winces in pain at Tanzy's manipulation of his neck. He again loosens his ascots.

> TANZY (CONT'D)
>
> Are you hurting?

Zipp shakes his head no.

> Please listen to me. I have to speak with you my love.

Zipp relents and turns his attention toward Tanzy. He sits on a chair watching her as she gracefully paces the room.

> My love, this four-year war is now over, and the years have bought us closer together, but we never discussed after the war and our plans.

She pauses and glances at him during her pace. She swallows hard.

You have given me everything a poor woman could ever have. A man
with a job, highly thought of in the community and treated me like a
queen that both our ancestors come from, but I don't feel like a woman
because I haven't given you the children a good man deserves. You
need to have a legacy. I know we tried hard but nothing has worked.

Zipp interrupts.

> ZIPP
>
> It could be me you know. I don't know anything about my parents.

Tanzy contemplates this but ignores his assertion.

> TANZY
>
> If a woman can't give the man she loves the babies he wants, it hurts her
> inside. There's nothing you can do about it.

> ZIPP
>
> What about our wedding vows? In sickness and health, richer or poorer,
> and it didn't say anything about kids.

Tanzy places her hands on her hips and looks at Zipp sarcastically.

> TANZY
>
> The preacher did speak about children. Right now, I'm mad at God. How
> can He let me have all those babies from those slave masters? Get them
> stolen away from me and now when I love someone and he loves me, we
> can't make none!

Tanzy is weeping and Zipp attempts to console her by embracing her. Olive watches from the room in a corner
solemnly.

> That's why I have to go up north to Philadelphia. I want us to go. You can
> find work in the fields. I'll work for some body washing their clothes,
> cooking and cleaning but now they would have to pay us. Then I can look
> for my babies.

Zipp considers his thoughts before he speaks, looking around the room for answers. He looks in Olive's direction
and she jumps wondering if she has been detected but he looks right through her.

> ZIPP
>
> Tanzy you my wife, and I don't want you to be no body slave woman no
> more. Do you believe they are going give you time off to go look for your
> children? You going be so tired, you just want to go home, plus they are
> expecting you to take care of them white children, and care for them like
> they your own. I know you hurting but you have to think this through.

Tanzy becomes a little bit more determined in her pace and she begins packing and looks outside the window at various blacks in horse and buggies, or on foot heading out of town.

> TANZY
>
> You see, look outside, they all leaving!

She points at the pedestrians heading in different directions with all their worldly possessions. Zipp comes over to the window and looks out with her.

> ZIPP
>
> You right, but everybody going in different directions and some not moving at all.

> TANZY
>
> Then why you packing?

The question stuns Zipp, after a long pause he leaves the window and goes back to packing. Tanzy remains at the window looking at him for an answer.   Zipp takes a deep breath.

> ZIPP
>
> I'm going south Tanzy, going back to Georgia.

Tanzy is incredulous and furious at the statement.

> TANZY
>
> Why? Why? Why? The Klansman tried to hang you there! I almost lost you there! That's a foolish idea to go back to the confederate state, who still want to make people slaves! I'm glad you taught me to read, because now I see how they use the bible to keep us down. No! No! You can't go!

Zipp lightly chuckles at Tanzy's advocacy. She takes offence to his laughter and she gives him a stern look.

> ZIPP
>
> Tanzy! I'm sorry for laughing at you and I love your concern, but I can't go North. This is the place I'm suppose to be.
> ZIPP (CONT'D)
>
> Where can an uneducated man get the education I received and a person that looks like me, earn the kind of money I made, get the respect I generated among white folks and black folks in Augusta, Georgia?

TANZY

Everybody didn't like you especially amongst the black folk, free and colored!

ZIPP

Yes, you are correct, but they like the parties I arranged. They drank the whiskey I supplied. They love the loans I provided when they needed to eat. I knew none of them could pay me back.

TANZY

But look how you got your money! You were in the lab, at the cemetery, and at the docks collecting body parts.

ZIPP

That's a part of my job. A part collecting barrels is where I found you.

There is silence as they both look at each other.

You know why I kept that Morse code machine? Every day at different times of day and night a message would come in and I send some out.

Tanzy nods her head in agreement.

My old job needs me back. The war is over. Medical schools still going to need new students. They going to need new bodies. Who you think is going to collect them? It will be different this time, because of the war there is 620,000 dead military people laying on the earth from the war. Now it's not just slaves, its whites too.

ZIPP (CONT'D)

God says everybody has to die. Where they go is up to them, but somebody has to pick up the shells. It might as well be me. I'm a scientist and that's what I know.

The couple continue packing in silence, after turning their backs to each other. Tanzy turns back to Zipp and he continues to pack different items in the house.

TANZY

I thought my husband with go with me, to protect me. You know a colored woman should be traveling alone.

Zipp, freezes his movements and he looks at her.

> ZIPP
>
> Somebody has to provide the money for you to travel, eat and live. That's why I have to get back to work. You're right, a woman traveling alone is bound to catch hell.

Tanzy stunned that Zipp agrees with her and she becomes a little excited that he might change his mind and go with her.

> ZIPP
>
> I have an idea!

EXT. ZIPP AND TANZY'S PLACE IN RURAL NORTH CAROLINA

Their buggy is packed with items and personal belonging. People are walking and riding in various directions. There is also a saddled horse with packed provisions for a loan rider. The buggy and the pack horse also have rifles attached.

On the steps of their place, Zipp and a soldier are standing there and the soldier leans down and kisses Zipp on the mouth. This act catches the walking onlookers by surprise and they walk onward and still continue to evil-eye the couple. The kiss breaks and Zipp walks the loan horse as the soldier walks to the buggy, then they switch places.

> ZIPP
>
> I told you it would work! The people think you're a man. No one is going to bother a 6'1 Union Solider, especially a war hero. Only you and I know. Keep the secret.

Tanzy gets up on the horse differently than a man would, and Zipp jumps on to the buggy.

> TANZY
>
> I'm afraid Zipp, I don't know how to be a man!

Zipp grabs the reins of the buggy preparing to dash.

> ZIPP
>
> I'm not asking you to be a man, it's impossible. I just need you to be a soldier and find your children.

Tanzy holds up her hands to make Zipp pause from taking off. Both of their eyes are watering at the actions of the pending departure. Olive comes down the steps and stands in the middle of the couple, uncertain who she should link her allegiance.

> TANZY
>
> I'm afraid. I have not seen my children in 20 years. They might not know me or I might not know them.

> ZIPP
>
> Would you rather stay in a known hell than an unknown heaven? You have to go, but just go slow!

Tanzy is about to say something but the emotions from Zipp takes over and he drops his head, snaps the reins on the buggy and jets down the road. The sudden bolt of the buggy stirs the lone horse, forcing Tanzy to hold the horse from bolting or throwing her to the ground. She turns and sees Zipp and the buggy dust down the road. She wipes away her tears, settles herself and trots in the opposite direction.

Olive still standing on the edge of the steps glancing back and forth follows the path of Tanzy.

Moments later the back of the buggy hits a bump in the road and uncovers part of the large mirror. In that same instance, Zipp in his frustration, anger, and disappointment snatches off his ascot revealing the noose scar from the near hanging that has swelled. It is infected and hurts to touch as he lightly daps at the drops of pus and blood. He discards the blood tinged ascot and rewraps it with another one and continues his journey.

EXT. OPEN FIELD 5 DAYS LATER AFTERNOON.

Tanzy is walking on the soft mud land and Olive is walking beside her. She is holding on to the rein of the horse who is trailing them.   Tanzy climbs a little hill and she steps into more soft mud but it oozes out spilled blood mixed with dirt and mud. She picks up her feet trying not to step in any more blood tinged mud, but it remains unavoidable as she climbs the hill. Olive stops cold. The horse pauses and fights climbing up the hill. She pulls back on the bit in her mouth and Tanzy has to fight with her to calm down as she yanks her up to the top of the hill.

At the top of the hill the sun is setting and a beautiful skyline, which captures Tanzy's attention. Yet, saturated on the grounds as far as she can see are littered bodies of union and confederate bodies. All of the bodies are decomposing. Some of the bodies are obliterated with body parts spread all over along with military equipment. Olive approaches the hill and reaches the top and looks across the land, ignoring the sun set. Olive's eyes are darting to and from as the spirits of death dart in and out of bodies searching for something that has life. She also witnesses some spirits flowing upward and out of sight. Olive stands at the beginning of the massacre as Tanzy and her horse wade through the carnage. Without warning the death spirits being running across the land, freeze and turn their heads toward Olive. She looks away and she looks back as they have moved closer. Olive takes a step back looking at Tanzy who is on her horse wading through and out of the corner of Olive's eye. She sees Tanzy reading and speaking words of the bible out loud. None of the spirits approach Tanzy's space. Those same spirits continually to move closer to Olive. Olive turns and begins trotting down the hill, distancing herself from the spirits. Olive looks over her shoulder and sees the dozens of the spirits of death chasing at top speed. She reaches the bottom of the hill and looks at the top of the hill. They are slowly descending the hill but with difficulty. Olive picks up speed and dashes down the road in Zipp's direction.

INT. MCG-LAB NIGHT DAYS LATER

Zipp is dressed in his lab coat. The lab is just as he left it. However, as Zipp lights a lantern to illuminate the lab, the room is filled with more barrels. There are also bunk-beds filled with cadaver of deceased soldiers. Zipp scans the room and there are bodies everywhere. Zipp examines the specimens of whites, blacks, Latino, and Chinese American soldiers from the civil war. Zipp begins his routine of logging in bodies and preparing each cadaver for dissection.

INT. ZIPP'S SHACK RIGHT BEHIND THE LAB. NIGHT

Olive walks around the room looking for Zipp. She looks out of the front window and sees the light in the lab and knows Zipp is working. She survey's the room, not looking at anything in particular and she goes on Tanzy's side of the room just admiring Tanzy's things brought back by Zipp. She sees nothing of significance and turns around and sees herself looking at the floor mirror that's been uncovered and set up as Tanzy would have enjoyed. It frightens her initially. She looks around cautiously. She hesitates and fingers around the edge of the mirror. During her hesitation, the front door opens and Zipp walks in. He is in obvious pain holding his neck and ripping off his ascot and tossing in to a pan with other blood and pus-soaked ascots. Olive moves away from the mirror and backs away as Zipp runs and stands directly in front of the mirror, examining his neck. During the self-examination of Zipp's neck, the swelling has ballooned quite large and is affecting Zipp's breathing. He is out of breath, choking and falls into the mirror splitting the mirror with chards of glass spreading across the room. Olive is stunned by the mishap. Olive watches Zipp claps his neck, choke, bleed, swallow his own blood and slowly lose consciousness. Olive slowly steps over Zipp's body and looks at the broken mirror pieces to squeeze her frame into the future generation. Olive takes a step into the broken mirror, while looking back at Zipp who is recovering consciousness.

INT. CAPITOL BUILDING BATHROOM MOMENTS LATER

Olive looks at her hands and is still mystified as she sits on the floor. Her hands spread. Olive then stands and walks toward the shattered mirror, climbs over the debris and enters the mirror. The door of the bathroom falls to the ground. Opesh, Rope' and security enters the bathroom. Olive fingers the floor, then stands. Security takes out handcuffs as Opesh grabs Olive by her shoulders and shakes her.

OPESH

What is wrong with you? You have jeopardized your job!

Olive slowly pulls away from Opesh and before security can take her away, she secretly places the ring in Opesh's hand. Opesh is shocked and speechless. Rope's comes over. Security snatches Olive away.

ROPE'

What happened? I never heard you shut up like that before?

Opesh shows Rope' the ring and she grabs it and holds it up to the light examining it.

ROPE' (CONT'D)

It's definitely yours.

Opesh heads out the door followed by Rope' looking back at the bathroom.

ROPE' (CONT'D)

Where are we going and what about this mess?

OPESH

I need to see what this woman is really about. We have the greatest insurance in the world, the United States of America.

EXT: THE CAPITOL BUILDING BOTTOM STEPS. EARLY MORNING.

Olive is on her knees with a toothbrush, a bucket and is scrubbing each individual step as media coverage surround her.

TELEVISON REPORTER

Miss why and how long are you going to be cleaning the Capitol Building steps with a tooth brush?

OLIVE

Until the truth is unspun. Until all my daughters come home whole.

EXT. CEDAR GROVE CEMEMTARY DAY 1986

The cemetery is in a disarray from years of neglect. Various headstones are crumbling and the dirt permanently disrupted.

There are a few people surrounding a caretaker who is showing them a map of the cemetery but he pointing in various directions. He motions to the map then shrugs his shoulders and also indicates he is clueless in what direction for them to proceed.

The few people in various directions attempt to read the map, which is difficult to read on the paper. Both ball up the map and drop in the various trash cans that are scattered throughout the cemetery, although the litter from the neighborhood has blown various debris on to the cemetery.

The people head for the exit and depart from the cemetery. As they close the gate, buried deep in a corner is a partial buried wooden headstone. On the front of the headstone that cannot be completely seen because of time are the letters in capitals ZIPP. Underneath the headstone are other headstones scattered over the years. Nothing in the cite is definitive.

THE END